POST-HOLOCAUST CHRISTIANITY

Paul van Buren's Theology of the Jewish-Christian Reality

James H. Wallis

University Press of America,® Inc.
Lanham • New York • Oxford

Copyright © 1997 by
University Press of America,® Inc.
4720 Boston Way
Lanham, Maryland 20706

12 Hid's Copse Rd.
Cummor Hill, Oxford OX2 9JJ

Library of Congress Cataloging-in-Publication Data

Wallis, James H.
Post-Holocaust Christianity : Paul van Buren's theology of Jewish-
Christian reality / James H. Wallis
p. cm.
Based on the author's thesis--Claremont Graduate School.
Includes bibliographical references and index.
l. Van Buren, Paul Matthews, 1924- Theology of the Jewish-
Christian reality. 2. Judaism (Christian theology) 3. Theology,
Doctrinal. I. Title.
BT78.V283W35 1997 231.7'6--dc21 97-33540 CIP

ISBN 0-7618-0899-X (cloth: alk. ppr.)
ISBN 0-7618-0900-7 (pbk: alk. ppr.)

Contents:

Chapter Two   35

Judaism's Attitude Towards Christianity

Chapter Three

Christianity's Attitude towards Judaism   53

Chapter Four

Van Buren's Methodology and an Argeument for a Theology of the Jewish-Christian Reality

Chapter Five

A Theology of the Jewish-Christian Reality: Van Buren's Worldview

Preface

This work is essentially a reworking of my dissertation at the Claremont Graduate School. I want to thank my committee members — John Roth, William Beardslee, and D.Z. Phillips — for their support and encouragement throughout the writing process. John Hick was an important teacher for me at Claremont, and indeed he chaired my dissertation committee before his retirement and return to England; so I wish to thank him, as well.

I can trace the origin of my interest in the Jewish-Christian dialogue back to a course (Romans) I had with Krister Stendahl while at seminary. Indeed, it was that course which set me on a path that finally led to this present work. But even more, it was Stendahl's course on Romans that has set me on the life-long task of not only trying to understand my Christian faith most importantly in terms of Judaism, but also in terms of all the other great religions of the world.

In 1987 I was a fellow of the Seminar in Jerusalem, which was sponsored jointly by the National Conference of Christian and Jews Inc. (N.Y., N.Y.) and the Shalom Hartmen Institute for Advanced Judaic Studies, (Jerusalem). There were twenty fellows (ten Christians and ten Jews) and our tesk was to study texts in the Tanakh, the Second Testament, and the Talmud on the theme of the covenant. The seminar was an enormously important and significant experience for me, as was the trip to Israel itself. It was an experience I shall never forget.

The director of the Seminar in Jerusalem was Paul M. van Buren. It was at the seminar that I became aquainted with Paul and his work. Indeed, it was because of the seminar that I decided to write my dissertation on Paul's contribution to the Jewish-Christian dialogue, his view of Christianity, Post-Holocaust. I have a great deal of gratitude and admiration for Paul M. van Buren; he is a fascinating Christian thinker. Obviously, the present work would not exist without him.

Finally, I want to thank Lori Gallinger who was an enormous help in getting this manuscript ready for publication.

INTRODUCTION

This work is concerned with Paul M. van Buren's contribution to the Jewish-Christian dialogue. Van Buren came to the dialogue late in his career. Thus, while his effort in the Jewish-Christian dialogue is the main focus of this work, we feel we must be concerned with his work prior to coming to the dialogue as well. Chapter One deals with van Buren's earlier work. The purpose of Chapters Two and Three is to set the stage for van Buren's work in the Jewish-Christian dialogue (1) by outlining how Judaism has viewed Christianity and how Christianity has viewed Judaism before the dialogue, and (2) by giving some sense of the dialogue leading up to van Buren. We do this by selecting the work of three representative participants in the dialogue from each side: Franz Rosenzweig, Martin Buber, and Han Joachim Schoeps on the Jewish side, and James Parkes, A. Roy Eckardt, and Rosemary Ruether on the Christian side. Chapter Four presents van Buren's argument for the need for a theology for the Jewish-Christian reality. The argument makes a unique contribution to the Jewish-Christian dialogue. The chapters that follow, Chapters Five, Six, Seven, and Eight are concerned with van Buren's "A Theology of the Jewish-Christian Reality," a systematic rethinking of Christianity vis-a-vis

Judaism.   The final chapter, Chapter Nine, contains both a critical
assessment of van Buren's contribution to the Jewish-Christian dialogue, as well as our own efforts at a contribution.   The purpose of
what follows is to introduce van Buren to the reader.

An Intellectual Biography of Paul M. van Buren.

Paul M. van Buren was a student of Karl Barth at the University of
Basel from 1951 to 1954.   His dissertation was on the Atonement in
Calvin.   It was published in 1957 with the title, *Christ in Our Place*,
and with a brief introduction by Karl Barth.   We might call this period
of van Buren's career his Barthian period.

After leaving Basel and returning to the United States van Buren
continued to be interested in the problems of classical Christology (van
Buren 1968, 20), which is evident in his next book, *The Secular
Meaning of the Gospel* (1963).   Still, the focus of this work is quite
other than classical Christology.   It is an attempt to present the Gospel
without the use of God-talk, and as such represents quite a departure
from the kind of work he was doing under his former teacher.   Indeed,
van Buren tells us that the book itself represented for him an important
step in his struggle to overcome his own theological past (van Buren
1968, 20) Still he never really explains his need to revolt against Barth.
At one point he simply says that the theological circle in which he was
functioning was becoming for him increasingly unreal (van Buren
1968, 20).

At any rate, what van Buren does in his revolt against his former
teacher is to turn to a method, linguistic analysis, which he finds in
Analytic Philosophy, a type of philosophy practiced in England and the
United States.   His concern now is to move the context of theology
from that of the church (Barth's understanding of the proper context of
theology) to that of contemporary culture (van Buren 1968, 21).   His
choice of linguistic analysis as a method of doing theology in this new
context seems to be based on the influence that some thinkers using
this method were having on his own thinking (van Buren 1968, 5-6).

Van Buren's effort in what he himself came to refer to as analytic
philosophy of religion, an effort that began with *The Secular Meaning
of the Gospel*, ended some twelve years later in a book called *The
Edges of Languages,* published in 1972.[1]   Why van Buren ended his
effort in this area with this work, he himself explains:

> With *The Edges of Language* I had reached the limits of what I could do to understand religion with the help of the work of Ludwig Wittgenstein, and I was not impressed with the results. I was not impressed with the results which others had come up with either. Some were cleverer than others, but none of them seemed to make much of a difference. Philosophers in general--and so also philosophers of religion--were simply writing for each other, and their results seemed to me to have little to do with the real world. (van Buren 1981, 67)

At this point van Buren, finding himself somewhat at loose ends, turns to administrative work. He teaches in the religion department at Temple University in Philadelphia, and in 1974 becomes its chairperson. During his time as chairperson the department needed to make two appointments in Judaism. It was in taking part in the process of making these appointments that van Buren discovers Judaism. He describes his discovery this way:

> Rosenzweig, importantly, but also all those other contacts with the world of Jews and Judaism, opened my eyes to something I had been looking at somewhat casually all along but had never really seen: Israel, the Jewish people, the people of God, was definitely alive. "The synagogue," "Jewish legalism," and all those old slogans of our theological tradition came tumbling down like the house of cards they were. In their place, actual Judaism, the living faith of this living people of God, came into view. (van Buren 1981, 69)

Unlike many Christian participants to the Jewish-Christian dialogue who came to it out of a recognition that it was the anti-Judaic tradition of the church that had a lot to do with the Holocaust occurring, van Buren comes to the dialogue out of his own personal discovery of "the living faith of this living people of God." This discovery is at the same time for van Buren a discovery that church teaching about Judaism is wrong. It is to correct this error, van Buren tells us, that has drawn him back into the work of theology and into the Jewish-Christian dialogue (van Buren 1981, 69). His contribution to this dialogue is to be found in his three volume set, *Discerning the Way* (1980), *A Christian Theology of the People Israel* (1983), and *Christ in Context* (1988), each with the subtitle, "A Theology of the Jewish-Christian Reality."

For van Buren a return to systematic theology is also a return to God-talk. God-talk had been for him a problem throughout his analytic philosophy of religion period. During that period, as we shall see, he attempted to solve the problem in different ways. He explains how he was able to move from the one position--seeing God-talk as a problem — to the position of simply using God-talk language, this way:

> Whatever my earlier difficulties in understanding the use of the word "God," I found that if I were to get anywhere with the problems now confronting me, I had to accept myself as a member of one of those two linguistic communities and therefore to speak with them of the God of whom they both spoke. My older problems did not receive any direct answers. They simply receded into the background; or rather, the position from which I had been asking them was no longer one on which I could stand if I were to take seriously the new (or very old) problem.
>
> Instead, seen from within this tension between the church and the Jewish people, what before had been the problem of "God" now was the problem of God as the God of both of these realities. By entering into their common problem and conflict, I found myself able and willing to speak their language. All the old problems remained, but they now appeared to be philosophical problems, not half so burning as the theological ones. I had run into a paradox and an incoherence that made the philosophical ones seem positively trivial. (van Buren 1981, 69-70)

In other words, the problem changes for van Buren. The one problem, the problem of talk of God, is a problem not even addressed by the other problem, the problem of God as God of both the Jewish people and Christians. They are different problems. The problem of God-talk is not solved by taking up the other; it remains a problem. Van Buren simply puts it down and picks up the other because for him now the Jewish-Christian problem is the more important one.

We might characterize van Buren's activity this way: He began as a student of Barth; *Christ in Our Place* represents this period. Then for perhaps twelve years his activities are in the area of analytic philosophy of religion; *The Secular Meaning of the Gospel* and *The Edges of Language* represent this period. And finally, van Buren returns to systematic theology with a concern for the Jewish-Christian dialogue.

Chapter One

Van Buren's Pre-Theology of the Jewish-Christian Reality Period

1. Van Buren's early theological position: *Christ in Our Place.*

Van Buren tells us in the Foreword to *Christ in Our Place* why he chose to write on Calvin. He believes that while Calvin had a great influence on the church in his own day, since then he has been misunderstood, hidden behind the veil of Calvinism. So van Buren wants to pull away the veil and show the real Calvin. To do this his method is mainly to let Calvin speak for himself. But van Buren also gives two other reasons for choosing to do his doctoral dissertation on Calvin: (1) because he admired the order and clarity of Calvin's work, (This is interesting because, as we shall see, the pursuit of clarity seems to be what motivates van Buren throughout his analytic philosophy of religion period.), and, (2) because he had a sense of dissatisfaction with Calvin. Our purpose in investigating van Buren's *Christ in Our Place* is to discovery where van Buren agrees with Calvin and where he disagrees with him, in order to get some idea as to what the theology of van Buren is at this early stage in his career.

1.1 Christocentrism and Anti-Judaism.

Let us begin with where van Buren agrees with Calvin. For Calvin, Barth, and van Buren, the starting point of theology is christology, which is to say, everything is seen from a christocentric perspective; Christ is the normative and sufficient revelation of God (van Buren 1957, vii, 8, 12, 76, 77, 141, 144). This christocentric position it should be noted does not allow room for Judaism, (nor for any other religion for that matter). Further, for Calvin, as for Christian theology in general as we shall see, anti-Judaism is a method of biblical interpretation for the purpose of Christian self-affirmation and self-definition. Let us give one example of Calvin's anti-Judaism that is also dealt with in van Buren's dissertation (van Buren 1957, 65-69).

According to Calvin, the sacrificial rites of ancient Israel were effective as promise and not as fact, i.e. they did not atone for sins at the time in which they were performed. They were worthless in terms of actually atoning for sins (fulfillment), but they were not worthless in terms of holding out a promise of eventual atonement. With the coming of Christ the promise was fulfilled. Still, Christ by fulfilling the promise of the ancient rites, did not negate them,[1] rather he affirmed their validity. Indeed, for Calvin the validity of the sacrifices continue. Nevertheless, while the ancient rites (the ceremonial law) remain meaningful and valid, they are no longer useful! The coming of Christ has abrogated not the effect of the cult of Israel, but the need any longer to practice that cult. The cult held out a promise; Christ's coming has fulfilled that promise. Its purpose has found satisfaction, and its use is ended (Calvin 1960, Book II, Chapter 7, section 16).

It should not surprise us that van Buren, as a student of Barth, should take the christocentric position of his teacher and of Calvin. Consequently, it should not surprise us either that when van Buren considers Calvin's interpretation of the ancient sacrificial rites of Israel, he does so without comment on the anti-Judaic nature of this interpretation. Perhaps it is because van Buren accepts the christocentric position of Calvin that he does not take a critical stand on Calvin's anti-Judaism. At any rate, the anti-Judaic tradition of the church is not van

Buren's concern at this point in his career; and therefore, it is also not where he disagrees with Calvin.

1.2 Calvin's Doctrine of the Atonement.

Just as van Buren accepts the christocentric position of Calvin, so also does he accept Calvin's understanding of the fallen nature of humanity. Because of sin, which Calvin understands as disobedience, all human beings are under the just punishment of death. Further, they are cut off from God, and there is nothing that they can do to return themselves to a right relationship with God. If there is any help for humanity, it must come from God (van Buren 1957, 65-69).[2]

Help for humanity comes by God the Father sending His eternal Son, Jesus Christ, the Incarnation into the world. The Incarnation is both human and divine, the two natures distinct but inseparable, united in one person (van Buren 1957, 20-21). The incarnational christology of Calvin, van Buren claims, is classical Christology that goes back at least to Irenaeus. Van Buren does not have a problem with this christology per se, which is to say, van Buren also at this point in his career holds to an incarnational christology. The problem van Buren does have is with the way the Incarnation is involved in redemption as that involvement is expressed by Calvin; and, according to van Buren, by every theologian before him stretching as far back as Irenaeus. We will need to explain van Buren's disagreement with classical Incarnational christology in this regard. But first let us continue mapping van Buren's agreement with Calvin's doctrine of the Atonement.

Christ takes the place of all human beings. He first takes our place by being obedient to God, where all are disobedient. He also takes our place by taking on the just punishment for our sins; he dies for us. Death is the punishment for sins. If Christ was obedient to God and yet suffered the punishment of death, then it was not for his sins he died, but for ours. He took our place, suffering the punishment that we deserved. This means we are no longer subject to the punishment, the debt being paid by Christ. So now we are reconciled to God, but not in ourselves, rather in Christ. In Christ we stand before God, because Christ in our place removed our sins; and in Christ we stand before God righteous, because Christ in our place was righteous (obedient) (van Buren 1957, 78-79).

This in summary is Calvin's doctrine of the Atonement; Christ in our place, Christ as our substitute. But this is also van Buren's view. That is to say, van Buren believes that Calvin's view fits best the biblical witness to the work of Christ (van Buren 1957, 142).

Let us now turn to van Buren's disagreement with Calvin. There are essentially two things about which van Buren disagrees with Calvin: (1) the involvement of God in the work of salvation, and (2) the scope of the salvation won by the work of Christ.

1.3 Van Buren's criticism of Calvin's Christology.

In terms of (1), we might put the issue this way: When Christ is on the Cross suffering the punishment due us because of our sins, what is being revealed on the face of Christ? For van Buren, what is being revealed is God, and because the face reveals one who is suffering, what is revealed is a God who suffers, a God who suffers for us (van Buren 1957, 39, 84). For Calvin, the suffering of Christ on the Cross is not the suffering of Christ in his divine nature, but only in his human nature. This is so because for Calvin, as for classical Christology in general, there is the belief in the impassibility of Christ's divinity. During Christ's suffering the divine nature rests passively and does not share in the work of Christ's human nature; the divine nature is hidden and not revealed on the Cross (van Buren 1857, 38-39, 49, 84).

Van Buren maintains that Calvin's position here is not consistent with the fundamental belief that van Buren shares with Calvin, namely that Jesus Christ is the full and complete revelation of God. For Calvin, what is revealed on the Cross is the suffering of a human being; for van Buren, it is the suffering of God. Calvin, somewhat inconsistently, holds to the impassibility of the divine nature of Christ and to the full and complete revelation of God in Jesus Christ. Van Buren, wishing to be more consistent than Calvin, is willing to give up the impassibility belief and to see God as a God who suffers (van Buren 1957, 141).

1.4 Van Buren's criticism of Calvin's Doctrine of Double Predestination.

The other disagreement that van Buren has with Calvin is in the belief as to what the work of Christ has accomplished. Has the work of

Christ accomplished the realization of our salvation, or the possibility of our salvation? We can put the issue this way: Suppose there is a kingdom in which all the subjects are slaves, and the king decides to free them. Now the question is as follows: When are the slaves free? Are the slaves free when the king signs the decree, or when messengers are sent, and individuals hearing the message believe it and begin behaving no longer like slaves, but like free persons? According to van Buren, Calvin chooses neither the one (when the king signs the decree, which is universalism), nor the other (only those are saved who hear and believe the message, which is limited atonement). Instead, Calvin leaves the two in tension: Christ is the reality of our salvation, but he is this only as we are related to him by faith (van Buren 1957, 103).

But the issue does not rest here. This is so because for Calvin this tension — Christ died for everyone, but not everyone is to be save — is viewed under the aspect of God's eternal election. God has elected some to salvation and some to damnation; this is Calvin's doctrine of Double Predestination.

Van Buren disagrees with Calvin's doctrine of Double Predestination. The work of Christ was done for everyone, and this is true whether anyone knows it or not, according to van Buren (van Buren 1957, 104). Still, van Buren does not move from this statement to the statement that everyone will be saved; he does not take the position of universalism. Instead, he moves from the statement that Christ died for everyone to the statement that all might be saved; "...we must maintain an eschatological suspension of knowledge and judgment about the ultimate decision of God in the case of any particular man" (van Buren 1957, 104). In other words, for van Buren who will and who will not be saved is not based on an eternal decision of God before the world began, but rather is based on God deciding each individual case at the Last Judgment. For Calvin, some are saved and some are damned (more precisely, few are saved, and most are damned). For van Buren, it is at least possible that God might work it out that all are saved.

For Calvin, if you are one of the elect then you will come to faith in Jesus Christ at some point in your life. Without faith one is lost, so if you are one of the elect God will bring it about that you will come to faith before you die; it is not possible to come to faith after death. Something similar to this is also true for van Buren. If God determines who will have ultimate salvation at the Last Judgment, a determining factor in God's decision will be whether one has or does not have faith in Jesus Christ. In other words, for van Buren as for Calvin and Karl Barth, faith in Jesus Christ is essential for salvation. This of course would lead one to ask this of van Buren: If God wills the salvation of everyone, and this we suggest is behind van Buren's disagreement with Calvin's doctrine of Double Predestination, why would God limit God's ability to do this by working only through Christianity?

1.5 *Summary of van Buren's early theology.*

Let us summarize van Buren's early theology as it is reflected in *Christ in Our Place.* Van Buren begins his career, literally and figuratively, as a pupil of Barth; furthermore, his doctoral dissertation under his teacher reflects this. Most importantly perhaps, van Buren shares the christocentric perspective of Calvin and Barth. This perspective views things out of the belief that the full and complete revelation of God is to be found only in Jesus Christ. This perspective leaves no room for Judaism (or for any other religion for that matter); Christianity is the one true religion. Knowing this, it is not surprising that van Buren does not take a critical stand towards Calvin's anti-Judaic interpretation of Scripture. The anti-Judaic tradition of the church is not an issue with van Buren at this point in his career.

Van Buren's disagreement with Calvin is relatively slight in comparison with his agreement with Calvin. Van Buren essentially agrees with Calvin's doctrine of the Atonement. His one reservation is the role the impassibility of God plays in it; a reservation that seems to be based on that belief being inconsistent with the christocentric perspective. For van Buren, Jesus on the Cross reveals a God that suffers for us. In this van Buren differs from Calvin and classical Christology. Van Buren's disagreement with Calvin's doctrine of Double Predestination perhaps has behind it the belief that a loving God must will to save everyone. At any rate, van Buren replaces divine election before all time with divine decision at the end of time, where it becomes the case that it at least might be that all are saved. Still, this does not move van Buren outside the circle of his christocentrism. If one is to be saved, it will only be through faith in Jesus Christ.

2. Van Buren's view of Christianity without God: a secular Christianity.

There are incredible changes from the van Buren *of Christ in Our Place (CIOP)* to the van Buren of *The Secular Meaning of the Gospel (SMG)*. In *CIOP*, van Buren's focus was on salvation seen from a christocentric perspective. In *SMG*, the focus is on rescuing the language of Christianity from meaninglessness. In *CIOP*, the dominant, perhaps the only influence on van Buren's thinking, was Karl Barth, his teacher. In *SMG*, Barth is still influencing him, but now there are other influences as well, and the dominant influence is now not Barth, but analytic philosophy, and more specifically its method of linguistic analysis. In *SMG*, van Buren believes he must present a secular Christianity, which means for van Buren a Christianity in which the word "God" is not to be found. We shall begin our investigation of *SMG* by attempting to understand why van Buren believes that this is what is needed.

2.1 Why a Secular Christianity?

We might categorize van Buren's reasons for the need to present Christianity in a secular way in two ways: (1) general cultural reasons, and (2) more specific philosophical reasons. The culture to which van Buren wishes to address his interpretation of Christianity is the English speaking culture of England and the United States, the culture to which he himself belongs. He believes that persons in this culture are secular persons, persons that think empirically and pragmatically. He further describes the secular person this way:

> Whatever ancient man may have thought about the supernatural, few men are able today to ascribe "reality" to it as they would to the things, people, or relationships which matter to them. Our inherited language of the supernatural has indeed died "the death of a thousand qualifications.

> The New Testament is mythological in that it pictures the world as having three stories, with heaven above and the realm of the dead below. Divine action is conceived as an intervention in this world by heavenly, transcendent powers. But men today can no longer give

credence to such a way of thinking. The scientific revolution, with its resulting technological and industrial developments, has given us another, empirical, way of thinking and of seeing the world. That which cannot be conceived in terms of man and the world explored by the natural sciences is simply without interest because it is not "real." (van Buren 1963, 4-5)

There was a time when Christians believed that God both transcended the world (creation) and yet was present to the world (immanentism) and capable of intervening in it. This the modern secular person does not believe, according to van Buren. Reality for secular persons is "...the things, people, or relationships which matter to them." Secular persons' reality is what can be conceived in terms of them and their world, and what can be explored by the natural sciences.

The *SMG* was written in the 1960s, and because of this book van Buren was associated with the "Death of God" theologians of the period. But van Buren claims that that association was not made by him but by others based on their own reading of his book (van Buren 1976, vii-viii). We will want to determine what van Buren's view on God's existence is in *SMG*. At this point what we know is that he does not believe that God intervenes in the world. But before considering what van Buren thinks about the existence of God, let us first consider what he thinks about the word "God." This consideration speaks to the philosophical reasons for which van Buren believes a secular interpretation of Christianity is called for.

Perhaps the best place to begin is where van Buren himself begins, with a parable by Anthony Flew, a British philosopher:

Once upon a time two explorers came upon a clearing in the jungle. In the clearing were growing many flowers and many weeds. One explorer says, "Some gardener must tend this plot." The other disagrees. "There is no gardener." So they pitch their tents and set a watch. No gardener is ever seen. "But perhaps he is an invisible gardener." So they set up a barbed wire fence. They electrify it. They patrol with bloodhounds...But no shrieks ever suggest that some intruder has received a shock. No movement of the wire ever betrays an invisible climber. The bloodhounds never give cry. Yet still the Believer is not convinced. "But there is a gardener, invisible, intangible, insensible to electric shocks, a gardener who has no scent and makes no sound, a gardener who comes secretly to look after the garden which he loves." At last the Sceptic despairs, "But what is left of your original assertion? Just how does what you call an invisible, intangible, eternally elusive gardener differ from an imaginary gardener or even from no gardener at all? (Flew 1955, 96)

Now, of course, the gardener in the parable is God, and what Flew hopes to show by the parable is that statements involving God, statements such as "God tends the garden," or more traditional Christian statements such as "God loves us," are meaningless because there is no way to determine whether they are true or false.

Analytic philosophy classifies statements this way: a priori analytic, a posteriori analytic, a priori synthetic, and a posteriori synthetic. It has generally placed assertions of logic and mathematics in the a priori analytic category. Also in this class are analytic statements such as 'All bachelors are unmarried.' Such statements are always true, such truth being determined by the meaning of the terms involved; or, said in a different way, analytic statements are true by definition. One would not have to consult the world in some way in order to determine the truth of an analytic statement; we might understand 'a priori' to have this meaning. The a posteriori analytic classification lacks any statements. If an analytic statement is true by definition, then there is no reason to consult the world to determine its truth. Suppose we did consult the world to determine the truth of, 'All bachelors are unmarried,' for example, and, suppose further that we found a person who claimed to be a bachelor but also claimed to be married. We would not conclude from this that we had found a counterexample to the statement, 'All bachelors are unmarried.' Rather, we would say that the person interviewed did not understand the meaning of the terms involved.

A posteriori synthetic statements are statements in which the world must be consulted in some way in order to determine whether they are true or false. A statement like, 'The table is red,' cannot be determined to be true by virtue of the terms involved; a table is not red by definition. In order to determine whether 'The table is red' is true or false one would have to look to see what color it is; one would have to consult the world in order to determine the truth or falsity of the statement.

Metaphysical statements and (some) religious statements are usually classed as a priori synthetic statements. These statements seem not to be determined by the meaning of the terms involved, yet they seem not to be determined by an appeal to the world either.

For Flew, only those (synthetic) statements that are capable of being verified or falsified empirically (by consulting the world in some way) are meaningful statements. Statements involving the word "God" are not capable of being verified in the desired sense, and so such statements are not meaningful; they are meaningless. In terms of Flew's parable the argument runs like this: If there is no state of affairs in the garden that could be obtained that would cause one to say that there is no gardener; then, the statement that there is a gardener is not a statement about the state of affairs in the garden; it is not a statement capable of being true or false; it is not a meaningful statement.

There seem to be two responses to Flew. One can maintain the cognitive nature of religious statements, statements like, "God loves us," by claiming that their verification is eschatological.[3] Or, one can take a noncognitive approach to the meaningfulness of religious language. Van Buren chooses the latter course.

For van Buren the word 'God' is not a word that refers to something. "It ['God'] seems to be a proper name, calling up the image of a divine entity, but it refuses to function as any other proper name does. Circumlocutions such as "transcendence," "being," and "absolute" only evade but do not overcome the difficulty" (van Buren 1963, 106 and 145). In other words, van Buren agrees with Flew that statements involving the word 'God' are not capable of being verified in an empirical way, and therefore are meaningless. But this does not mean that the language of faith is meaningless. It is language in which the word 'God' does not appear, and it is language in which its meaning is not determined by truth or falsity; it is noncognitive language.

2.1.1 Summary.

Let us review: For van Buren, secular persons are empirical and pragmatic. They do not believe that God intervenes in their world. Analytic philosophy, a discipline that is part of the world of secular persons, has shown that on empirical grounds statements in which the word 'God' is used are meaningless, i.e. not capable of being true or false. Van Buren wishes to save Christianity from meaninglessness, yet he also wishes to present a Christianity that speaks to secular people. This means for van Buren a Christianity that does not use the word 'God,' and a Christianity that uses noncognitive language, a secular Christianity.

2.2 Van Buren's position on the Existence of God.

Before turning to van Buren's secular Christianity, let us first ask the following: We already know that van Buren does not believe that God intervenes in the world. Does he believe that God exists at all? Now admittedly we have a problem in even asking the question. If any statement in which the word 'God' appears is a meaningless statement-- the word 'God' does not refer to anything (in the world)--then our question, Does van Buren believe that God exists? is meaningless. Granting this, van Buren nevertheless does give us some indication as to his approach to God's existence. In some places in *SMG* he seems to agree wtih T.R. Miles that the appropriate response when the question of God's existence comes up is that of silence (van Buren 1963, 92, 144, 148). This tells us nothing about what van Buren believes about God's existence, however. There is one place in *SMG* where he does explicitly state that he is agnostic about God's existence: "We are saying that it is possible today to be agnostic about "otherworldly" powers and beings..." (Van Buren 1963, 195).

2.3 A Secular Christianity; Building on the work of Hare,
Ramsey, and Braithwaite.

For van Buren in *SMG* the central problem facing Christianity is saving its language from meaninglessnes (van Buren 1963, 4). We now have some idea why this is so — the language of Christianity has essentially been God-talk. But analytic philosophers, who for van Buren represent the secular person's point of view, have shown that such talk is meaningless. Van Buren agrees that God-talk is meaningless, but does not agree that therefore the language of Christianity is meaningless. He believes that he can give an interpreta-tion of Christianity that will satisfy the secular person's criterion of meaningfulness; he believes he can give a secular meaning to Christianity. Van Buren's work builds on the work of R.M. Hare, Ian T. Ramsey, and R.B. Braithwaite. So let us begin by briefly considering the positions of these three analytic philosophers.

Hare rescues the language of Christianity from meaninglessness by claiming that such language is not cognitive; its meaning is not based on understanding the language as statements that are verifiably true or false. Religious language does not function in the same way as ordinary empirical statements. Rather, the language of Christians is an expression of a "blik," where a "blik" is a fundamental attitude, an orientation, a commitment to see the world in a certain way; and a way of life that follows upon this orientation. (van Buren 1963, 85-87). In other words, we are to understand religious language as language that says something about the persons who use such language — their attitude, orientation, and commitment. Such language is not about God, even if such language contains the word "God;" it is about human beings.

Ramsey's contribution to the noncognitive approach to religious language, at least as far as van Buren's own position is concerned, seems to be in supplying an explanation as how one acquires a "blik." Such language, according to Ramsey, points to certain kinds of situations, situations of disclosure when "the light dawns," and the situation becomes alive and new. Such experiences result in commitment, whereby what is "seen" in the disclosure or discernment becomes important and determines subsequent seeing. In other words, it is experiences which Ramsey characterizes as disclosure experiences which accounts for a person having a certain "blik" (van Buren 1963, 87 and 91).

The importance of Braithwaite for van Buren seems to be in two areas: (1) he elaborates further on how a "blik" is acquired, and (2) he gives a criterion for meaningfulness of religious language.

According to Braithwaite, besides a "blik" which he understands as an intent to behave in a certain way, religious persons will also entertain certain stories which are associated in the mind of the believers with their "blik." The stories function in the language of Ramsey as the disclosure experience which occasioned the acquiring of the "blik" associated with the stories. In other words, the stories cause the "blik" to occur in those to whom it does occur.

Are the stories true? In a sense they are, and in a sense they need not be. The sense of their truth is determined by whether they function in the way they are supposed to function. If the stories occasion the acquiring of the "blik" that is associated with them, then the stories are true. True, that is, for the ones for whom the stories have become the occasion of them acquiring the associated "blik". But, if the stories do not produce such an occasion, then they are not true. Not true, that is, for those for whom they have not become the occasion for acquiring the "blik" associated with the stories. The statements made within the stories need not be true, that is to say, need not correspond to empirical fact. In this way, the stories could be false — the statements in the stories do not correspond to empirical facts — yet true — true in the sense that they function in the way they are suppose to function; they occasion the acquiring of the "blik" associated with them (van Buren 1963, 92-96).

For Braithwaite, the criterion for the meaningfulness of Christian language is the intention of those using that language to follow a Christian way of life. The statement made by Christians that God is love, for example, translates according to Braithwaite's theory of meaning into a statement in which Christians declare their intention to follow a loving way of life; God-statements are translated into human statements (van Buren 1963, 94).

2.4 Van Buren's Secular Interpretation of Christianity.

With this brief consideration of the contribution of Hare, Ramsey, and Braithwaite to a noncognitive interpretation of religious language, we are now ready to consider van Buren's secular interpretation of the Gospel. If Christianity is not about God, then what is it about? It is about Jesus of Nazareth.

Van Buren begins by making it clear that the Jesus he shall be concerned with is the Jesus of history. By history van Buren means the answering of questions about human action in the past. And, by Jesus van Buren means a human being who has a place in the realm of human action in the past (van Buren 1963, 111). We might put it this way: Van Buren is concerned with Jesus as a human being who existed in the past; he is concerned with Jesus as a piece of history, seen from the perspective of history.

For van Buren the historical Jesus is to be defined in terms of freedom:

He was free from anxiety and the need to establish his own identity, but he was above all free for his neighbor. This was the characteristic which Bonhoeffer, in his last writings, found so impressive. He was free to be compassionate for his neighbor, whoever that neighbor might be, without regard to himself. The tradition reveals the impress of this characteristic with its frequent references to his compassion for those who suffered, his openness to all whom he met, his willingness to associate with those whose company was avoided by respectable people. He was reported to have taught that the greatness of freedom lies in service, and his own freedom was characterized by humble service to others. (van Buren 1963, 123) [4]

The historical Jesus is the definitive free person for those who take the Christian perspective, but he is not the occasion by which the perspective itself is acquired. For van Buren, this is another way of saying that the freedom of Jesus did not cause others to be more free or to share in the freedom that he had during his life-time. Rather, the freedom of Jesus becomes "contagious" only with Easter (van Buren 1963, 133).

For van Buren, it is with Easter that Peter and the other disciples begin to exhibit the freedom of Jesus, and it is with Easter that they acquire the Christian "blik":

It seems appropriate to say that a situation of discernment occurred for Peter and the other disciples on Easter, in which, against the back-ground of their memory of Jesus, they suddenly saw Jesus in a new and unexpected way. "The light dawned." The history of Jesus...took on a new importance as the key to the meaning of history.... From that moment, the disciples began to possess something of the freedom of Jesus. His freedom began to be "contagious." (van Buren 1963, 132 and 134)

But if the acquiring of the Christian "blik," as well as something of Jesus' freedom occurred to the apostles "against the background of their memory of Jesus," obviously this could not be the case for anyone who had no memory of Jesus. If this were the only way to acquire the Christian faith perspective, then it would seem that the Christian faith would be limited to those who knew Jesus during his life-time. But, of course, the Christian faith was not limited to Jesus' disciples. Rather, this is where the Gospel comes in, which we must understand as the story of Jesus entertained by those who had taken the Christian perspective. The disciples proclaimed the Gospel, and this became the occasion of acquiring the Christian "blik," as well as the entertaining of the same Gospel, for those for whom the hearing became an experience of discernment and disclosure. Such hearers also "caught" some of the freedom that the story of Jesus told them was the freedom that Jesus himself had. Indeed, the story was told by those who claimed that Jesus was a free person who had set them free, and could set the hearer free as well (van Buren 1963, 134).

Let us summarize van Buren's secular meaning of the Gospel. Jesus was free for others. On Easter that freedom began to be contagious. First Jesus' disciples caught it. They also acquired an attitude towards life of which Jesus was the norm. For the disciples the norm was their memory of Jesus; for later Christians the norm was the Gospel, i.e. the story about Jesus. The story functions as the occasion whereby one might acquire the Christian "blik," as well as some of the freedom that was Jesus'. The story also is something that is constantly entertained by those that hold to the Christian perspective on life.

Perhaps it might be interesting to consider how van Buren understands Jesus' death in terms of his secular interpretation of Christianity. Obviously the Atonement doctrine he held to *in Christ in Our Place* will not be consistent with a secular interpretation, an interpretation in which the only reality is an historical reality, a this-world reality. For van Buren, Easter is the event by which Jesus' freedom becomes contagious. Humans lack freedom, van Buren tells us, although he never addresses the origin of this lack. At any rate, the secular meaning of Jesus' death is this: he died so that others might share in the freedom that he enjoyed (van Buren 1963, 134, 137).

It is obvious also that in a secular meaning of the Gospel there would be no room for an after-life. What the resurrection of Jesus means in such an interpretation has to do with eschatology. What van Buren means by eschatology is that of the goal of all existence. The resurrection of Jesus expresses the Christian hope that the goal of all existence is to share in the freedom that Jesus had; that that freedom might prevail on earth (van Buren 1963, 154).

2.5 Secular Christianity and Other Religions.

Perhaps the biggest change from the van Buren of *Christ in Our Place* to the van Buren of *The Secular meaning of the Gospel* is from his use of the word "God" without question (an uncritical use of the word) to an interpretation of the Christian faith without the use of the word "God," a consistently secular or this-worldly interpretation of Christianity. But perhaps there is another change that is just as dramatic. In *CIOP* van Buren held the position which he shared with Calvin and Barth that salvation is only through faith in Jesus Christ. Now salvation in *SMG* certainly has a different meaning for van Buren than it had for him in *CIOP*. In *CIOP* salvation, or at least ultimate salvation, meant eternal life with God in the heavens. This in *SMG* is now meaningless language. In *SMG* salvation means freedom, human freedom in a human world. But the question is: Is "catching" the freedom that Jesus had the only way freedom can be acquired? Is Christianity the only true religion? Let us try to map van Buren's position on this point.

Van Buren's position on what we might call Christianity and other religions seems to be based on his desire to take a consistently empirical (secular) view of things. If the Christian perspective is acquired in the way it is, then,

> There is no empirical ground for the Christian's saying that something of this sort could not happen to a disciple of Socrates. Reading the history of Socrates might conceivably have a liberating effect on a person, who might say that he shared in the freedom of the philosopher. If this were to happen, the Socratic's freedom, presumably, would be defined by the peculiar character of Socrates' freedom. He would acknowledge Socrates as his norm. He would be "in Socrates," let us say, not "in Christ." (van Buren 1963, 138-39)

Here van Buren uses the example of acquiring a "blik" and sharing in the freedom of a philosopher, namely Socrates. It is clear that for van Buren what happens to one who becomes a Christian can also happen to one who reads a philosopher, but also it can occur by way of an ideology or by way of other religions (van Buren 1963, 155).

Van Buren's position on all the different perspectives on life, specifically religious or otherwise, is that they all make claims of superiority, but that such claims cannot be proven; that they all use exclusivistic language, e.g. "Christ is the only way," said by a Christian, but that such language functions to express the conviction with which the ones who use such language hold to what they say. Such language says something about those who use the language, but does not express some objective truth; such language does not involve empirical statements (van Buren 1963, 76, 139, 140, 155).

However, for van Buren the Christian faith perspective does not acknowledge the faith perspective of another, at least not in terms of the other's perspective. If Christians meet some persons, for example, that they perceive as free, they will understand them to have "caught" their freedom from Jesus, regardless of where those persons themselves may say they found their freedom (van Buren 1963, 142). Van Buren does not explicitly state that the reverse holds, but presumably it does, that is, that those of another perspective would view the Christian perspective in terms of their own perspective. For example, those "in Socrates" would view the freedom they perceive in Christians as having its source in Socrates.

It is not clear to us why a Christian must view the freedom of others in terms of Jesus and not in terms of the witness of the others as to the sources of their freedom. Even in terms of van Buren's own view, we do not see why a Christian could not acknowledge that just as there are other faith perspectives, there are different sources to those perspectives as well. Would the acknowledging of other sources to other faith perspectives by Christians diminish the conviction with which they hold to their own faith perspective? We don't think so.[5]

2.6 Christology.

In van Buren's secular interpretation of Christianity Jesus is viewed as a man, an exceptionally free man, whose freedom became contagious on Easter, and whose history, i.e. the Gospel, the story of Jesus, is the norm for the lives of those who have "caught" some of his freedom and have acquired the Christian "blik". But van Buren also feels a need to present a christology which he at least hopes will satisfy his former teacher, Karl Barth. He calls it a christology of "call" and "response".

Van Buren prefaces his "call" and "response" Christology with a criticism of the Chalcedonian Christology. In *Christ in Our Place* van Buren's criticism of the classical Christology was that it was inconsistent with the full and complete revelation of God in Jesus Christ. Holding to the impassibility of the divine nature, it taught that the divine nature of the Son was hidden and not revealed on the Cross. Van Buren's objection to it in *The Secular Meaning of the Gospel* is that it does not do justice to the humanness of Jesus.

The Chalcedonian formulation understands Jesus Christ as having two natures, a divine nature and a human nature, united in one hypostasis of the Logos. 'Hypostasis' might be translated as 'actuality' or 'existence'; it is what constitutes the actual or independent existence of something. What makes human beings actual human beings is their humanness; humanness is their hypostasis. The hypostasis of Jesus Christ, however, according to Chalcedon, is God the Word (the Logos). What this means is that Jesus Christ in actuality is God, God with a human nature and a divine nature. Jesus is not an actual human being; his existence is not constituted by his humanness (van Buren 1963, 38-40).

With this criticism van Buren rejects classical Christology as not being adequate to a contemporary articulation of the Christian faith. But he cannot make this claim based on a secular point of view because what he is attempting to do is to present a christology that would satisfy what he calls the theological "right," i.e. Barth. His secular interpretation of Jesus would certainly not be acceptable to the "right," but perhaps a christology based on insights of biblical theology would be (van Buren 1963, 47).[6]

Van Buren begins by giving a definition of "Son" or "Son of God" that is not based on patristic Christology but based on its meaning in the Bible:

> In calling him [Jesus] the Son of God, the apostolic community was saying that the true and faithful Israel had come. God had chosen him as his servant to participate in his plan for the world, to be (as the old Israel had not been willing to be) "a light to lighten the Gentiles." Jesus as "Son of God" meant Jesus as the obedient bearer of a specific election or commission (van Buren 1963, 48).

We shall begin by making three observations about this passage, and then develop them separately: (1) This christology is functional. It views Jesus as a man chosen by God to perform a certain role. (2) It is anti-Judaic, and (3) It involves God-talk.

The role to which God had called Jesus was to be the one through whom everyone else is to be faithful to God (van Buren 1963, 52). Jesus was a human being just like all other human beings, and the role to which he was called by God did not make him other-than-human (van Buren 1963, 53). Nevertheless, Jesus is unique. His uniqueness is defined by his calling, but also by his response to that call. He was the one man who truly existed for others, he was the only one who perfectly obeyed his calling; everyone else was disobedient (van Buren 1963, 53-54).

The view of Judaism that we find in this christology is the traditional Christian view of Judaism. Judaism's purpose is to prepare for the coming of Christianity. Once Jesus comes, Judaism's purpose is ended. Indeed, with the coming of Jesus Israel is no longer Israel, but the "old" Israel. Jesus and those that are faithful to God through him are the "new" Israel (van Buren 1963, 52-53).

This christology is involved in God-talk. God calls Jesus to a specific role in history, and Jesus responds to this call. He accomplishes that which was the purpose of God, namely, that only through Jesus is everyone to be faithful to God. What this means is that exclusivistic language will not be viewed as expressing the conviction with which believers hold their beliefs, but rather as expressing the purpose and actions of God.

The "call" and "response" Christology of van Buren is a christology which differs from the christology he held to in *Christ in Our Place* only in terms of Jesus. In CIOP Jesus is viewed ontologically, here he is viewed functionally. In CIOP he was viewed as the Word of God (the Logos), having both a divine and a human nature. Here Jesus is a man who was given a role by God, a role which he perfectly filled. But if the way in which Jesus is viewed has changed, nothing else has. Christianity by the action and purpose of God remains the only true religion, and anti-Judaism remains the theological means of Christian self-affirmation.

With the functional aspect of Jesus that van Buren presents in his "call" and "response" Christology, he might have presented a different Christianity. If it was not God God's self who came to earth to establish Christianity, but rather it was the man Jesus responding to a call of God, then perhaps God established other religions by working with other people. In other words, even with God-talk exclusivistic language could be understood as saying something about believers and not something about God. That van Buren does not move in this direction, we attribute to the continued Barthian influence upon him; his need to satisfy in his own theological thinking the position of his teacher.

The problem is that except for viewing Jesus as a man, van Buren's "call" and "response" Christology and his secular Christology are not compatible. As van Buren develops it, the Christianity that follows from the first leaves no room for other religions in general, and is anti-Judaic in particular. The Christianity that follows from the latter does allow for other faith perspectives, and theoretically at least this would include a Jewish faith perspective, although van Buren never specifically addresses the issue.   His secular interpretation of Christianity is not inherently anti-Judaic; he makes only one anti-Judaic statement in articulating it (van Buren 1963, 144). Nevertheless, there is no serious problem with this incompatibility. This is so because, while van Buren feels the need to give a christology in terms of Barth, this is not the christology that dominates his thinking. It is the secular view that predominates in *The Secular Meaning of the Gospel.*

Let us mention one further continuing influence of Barth on van Buren.   Van Buren interprets classical Christology in terms of his secular meaning of Christianity. To give but one example: In classical Christology the two natures of the Son are inseparably and indivisibly united. What this means in terms of van Buren's secular interpretation is that the Christian "blik" and the story of Jesus that those who have the Christian "blik" entertain, are inseparably and indivisibly united (van Buren 1963, 166). Such an interpretation seems forced, and we wonder what is gained by it.   For van Buren, it is fulfilling the responsibility a theologian has to Christian thought. Such a sense of responsibility van Buren inherited from Barth (van Buren 1963, 159).[7]

2.7 Summary of a Secular Christianity.

Let us attempt to summarize the focus of *The Secular Meaning of the Gospel.* It is van Buren's belief that Christians are secular people. What this means generally is that they are pragmatic and empirical in outlook, an outlook that excludes a God that intervenes in worldly affairs.   About the existence of God at all, the secular Christian is agnostic. Analytic philosophy, a discipline within our secular culture, demonstrates that God-talk is meaningless. Therefore, what is needed for Christianity is an articulation of the faith that does not speak of God. The meaning of Christianity is that it says something about those who hold it; it says nothing about God. Such a Christianity focuses on Jesus and on Easter.   Christians orient themselves to the world in a certain way; they have a certain perspective on life, the norm of which is the story of Jesus. This story also functions at least in some people to convert them to the Christian point of view. There are other points of view besides the Christian one. None of them can be proven to be the only true one. Nevertheless, Christians will view others who exhibit a sense of freedom as having caught their freedom from Jesus, regardless of what they themselves may say is the source of their freedom. Salvation is freedom, and the Christian hope is that freedom will prevail on earth. This does not mean that the Christian hope is that some day everyone will be Christian. What it does mean is that if (some day) everyone did exhibit freedom, then Christians would view that freedom as having its source in Jesus, regardless of what others might say.

Van Buren's view of other religions seems to be based on viewing them using the Christian norm, Jesus. Basically we do not see why van Buren could not have moved to the acceptance of the witness of others as to the source of their freedom. Why for Christians does the freedom of others have to be viewed in terms of Jesus? Why can't Christians acknowledge the witness of others as to the source of their freedom? We see nothing in van Buren's position that would prevent him from making this move. Nevertheless, it is not a move that he makes.

Finally, we might ask some questions of van Buren's secular view of Christianity. Can Christianity do without God-talk? If the use of the word "God" is a problem, is it a problem for ordinary Christians, as van Buren maintains?   Are Christians when they talk about their faith simply saying something about themselves and perhaps Jesus, or do they wish to say something more than that?   How important to Christianity is the belief in an after-life? Doesn't van Buren in *The Secular Meaning of the Gospel* give up too much of Christianity to secularism?[8]

3. A Theory of Religious Language for a Secular Christianity: The Edges of Language.

In *The Secular Meaning of the Gospel* van Buren was concerned to present a secular Christianity, an interpretation of Christianity without the use of the word "God," because it had no meaning. In *The Edges of Languages* van Buren's concern is with the nature of religious language. This work presents a theory of religious language in which a use for the word "God" is found. Nevertheless, as we shall see, the use of the word is not to say something about God, but rather to say something about those who use the word. In other words, just as in *The Secular Meaning of the Gospel*, van Buren in *The Edges of Language* will hold to a view of religious language in which what is said by those using the language expresses something about themselves, not something about God. Still, the theory of religious language that van Buren presents in *The Edges of Language* is quite different from that that he held to in *The Secular Meaning of the Gospel*.

Perhaps the best way to approach van Buren's theory of religious language is to consider an image he himself uses to help explain his theory, that of language as a platform (van Buren, 1972, 82-3).

Humans are distinctively linguistic beings, which is to say, we exist and live on a language platform. The planks of the platform are the rules for the use of words, the rules that govern our behavior as linguistic beings. The planks have been laid by social convention. The laying of more planks, or the replacement of old planks, i.e. the changing of the platform in any way, is a social act.

We are free to move on our language platform as we wish; it is our choice. But our choices have consequences. Where we are on the platform determines our linguistic behavior, what we do as linguistic beings. Near the center of the platform the rules for the use of words are relatively precise and clear. Thus it is near the center of the platform we would move if we wished our linguistic behavior to be clear, precise, and unambiguous. But we might also chose to move to the edges of the platform. What would our linguistic behavior be like there?

For van Buren, everyone begins at the center of the platform. This is so because to be at the edges of language is to have gotten there by pushing at the limits of the applications of words. In other words, language at the edges is language at the center that has been pushed, stretched, and strained to its limit, the edges of the platform. For van Buren, humor, love-language, poetry, aspects of metaphysics, and religious language are forms of walking the edges of language. We will restrict ourselves to considering Christian language in our attempt to understand what van Buren means by pushing words to the limit of the conventions for their usage, or, walking on the edges of language.

We have said that we are free to move anywhere on the platform we choose, but that we at least begin near the center. If this is true, then what would motivate us to move from the center, where the rules for the use of words are clear and familiar, to the edges, where the rules for linguistic behavior are not so well defined? The answer to our question is this: It is the result of a longing, an intensity of concern, a passion for some aspect of our linguistic existence (van Buren 1972, 111,115, and 120-1).

For van Buren, all religions share the feature of language stretched to its limits. What differentiates one religion from another is where the stretching occurs (van Buren 1972, 117). For Christianity the pushing and stretching occurs in the telling of what happened in the history of Jesus (van Buren 1972, 123).

Christian linguistic beings can find themselves at the center of the platform of language by saying such things as: Jesus was born at such and such a time in such and such a place by such and such parents. But Christians have been moved to want to say more than can be said about Jesus near the center of the language platform. They have been moved, for example, to say that Jesus' history continues after his death (resurrection), and that it will continue as long as there is any history at all. But this is stretching the talk of the history of someone almost beyond recognition, according to van Buren. It is pushing such talk (language about the history of a person) to the edges of language (van Buren 1972, 125).

Let us give just one other example of how a Christian pushes and stretches language at the center of the platform out to its edges. Just as we might say that there is an American way of life of which we could give a description, just so we might also say that there is a Christian way of life that could also be described. In both cases we would be using language near the center of the platform. But Christians would not be satisfied with saying that Christianity is a way of life. They would be motivated to say all that could possibly be said on the matter, because it is for them a matter of great concern. Such a motivation would cause them to push a statement like, 'Christianity is a way of life.' from its use near the center of the language platform out to its edges by saying such things as, 'Christianity is indeed a way of life, but it is also more than that. It is *the* life, the more abundant life, eternal life! It is life that presses on to what is more alive than life! It is life with God! (van Buren 1972, 157).

In *The Secular Meaning of the Gospel* van Buren could find no use for the word "God." Language in which the word was found was thus meaningless. Van Buren, in his attempt to protect Christian language from meaninglessness, presented a Christianity in which the word "God" was not found. In *The Edges of Language* van Buren finds a use for the word "God," and therefore language in which the word "God" is found is now meaningful language. But what exactly is its meaning? What does it mean, for example, that Christian life is life with God?

For van Buren, the word "God" functions as the boundary of what can be meaningfully said. To say more is to fall off the edge of the platform into nonsense, into meaninglessness. The use of the word "God" signals that we have reached the absolute limit of what can be meaningfully said, when we desperately want to say all that can possibly be said about something that is of great concern to us. The use of the word "God" by us as linguistic beings signals that we have reached the limit of our linguistic behavior. As such, it says something about us---we are engaged in linguistic behavior that signals we are at the limit of our language. It says nothing about God (van Buren 1972, 132-33).

"God" does not refer to God, or, one does not refer to God by use of the word "God". To think that the use of the word "God" is to refer to God, is a mistake that can occur by viewing language as made up of individual words that name objects; words are names that name the objects of which they are the names; "God" is a name that names the object, God. But the meaning of words is not simply that of naming. The meaning of some words, at any rate, is in the use to which they are put, the work that they do, which may be other than that of naming.[9]

First, we must remember that language use begins near the center of the platform. Religious language is ordinary language pressed and pushed and stretched to the edges. Second, the word "God" appears at the edges of language. It does not appear near the center. It is to think that religious discourse is like ordinary discourse, it is to think that religious language exists at the center of the platform and not at its edges, that leads to the mistake that "God" refers to God, that "God" is a name that names God.

Van Buren's notion is this: Christians begin at the center of the platform with the story of Jesus. But they are driven to say all that they can possibly say about him. They are driven to the edges of language. Some of the words that they found at the center of the platform, words like 'father' and 'power,' for example, words that are part of the Jesus story, are not adequate for what they want to say if used only as they are used at the center of the platform. So they stretch and push the use out to the edges where 'father' and 'power' become 'almighty Father.' But even this is not enough to satisfy the desire to say all they possibly can say about what is for Christians their greatest concern, the story of

Jesus. And so, they go to the absolute limit of what they can say, they say, "God".

But again, the use of the word "God" is not to refer to God, but to signal that the users have reached the ultimate limit of what they can say in their longing to say absolutely all that they possible can say about their Christian faith. "God" is a signal that the user has reached the outer edges of language; to move out further would be to fall off into nonsense. "God" says something about the users — it marks the limit of their linguistic behavior---it says nothing about God. "God" is a speech-act, a performative utterance, a piece of linguistic behavior that acknowledges the limits of speech. "God" does not function by referring to some object, but rather functions as a boundary marker as to what is linguistically possible; it marks the absolute limit of our linguistic existence.

If we now have some understanding of van Buren's theory of religious language and the place of the word "God" within that theory, let us now consider how van Buren's view has changed, and how it has not changed since *The Secular Meaning of the Gospel.*

In *The Secular Meaning of the Gospel* van Buren held that a God that intervenes in our lives was no longer believable, and his stand on the existence of God was agnostic. He continues to hold these views in *The Edges of Language* (van Buren 1972, 12, 13, 160). If he has found a use for the word "God" in *The Edges of Language* it has not been that of referring to God. The reason he finds a use for "God" is that he wishes to present a theory of religious language that captures a feature of religion which he says was lacking in his earlier view. That feature is the one of mystery, wonder, and awe (van Buren 1972, 43). It is this feature of religion that drives us to want to say as much as can possibly be said, that drives us to the edges of language, where, when we reach the absolute limit of what we can say, we say, God.

We might see the theory that van Buren presents in *The Edges of Language* as a further development of the theory he gave in *The Secular Meaning of the Gospel.* It is a theory of religious language for a secular Christianity. In *The Secular Meaning of the Gospel* Christians by their language express a certain orientation towards life, an intent to behave in a certain way, a commitment to a particular life-style, the Christian life-style. In *The Edges of Language* this way of viewing Christian language seems to be too near the center of the language platform. Emotion, we might say, is introduced that stretches and strains and pushes the language to its limit. We indicate that we have reached that limit when we say, God.

3.1 First Indications of an Interest in the Jewish-Christian Dialogue.

In *The Secular Meaning of the Gospel* van Buren was anti-Judaic, a victim, perhaps an unconscious victim, of the Christian anti-Judaic tradition. In *The Edges of Language* van Buren shows signs that he is moving towards the Jewish-Christian dialogue. In *The Secular Meaning of the Gospel* the history of Jesus was the culmination of the history of Israel. The "new" Israel, the church, begins where the "old" Israel leaves off, namely, with Jesus. In *The Edges of Language* Christians are not viewed as replacing Jews, but rather joining them. Indeed, Christians enter into Israel, becoming Jews themselves by adoption (van Buren 1972, 130). Exactly what this means we will discover when we consider van Buren's systematic view on the subject. As we shall see, he does not for very long hold to the view that Christians are adopted Jews. His reason is that it became obvious to him that Christians are for the most part Gentiles, and not Jews, not even adopted Jews. In other words, van Buren seems to have seen the implication for Christians of calling Christians adopted Jews. But, as we shall also see, he seems never to have recognized the implication for Jews of calling Christians adopted Jews.

4. Summary.

Van Buren began his career as a pupil of Barth. His dissertation, *Christ in Our Place,* reflects the fact that he was very much influenced by Barth. Indeed, it is not too much to say that van Buren's theology at this point in his life was shaped by the theology of Barth. God fully and perfectly revealed God's self in Jesus Christ. Everything is seen from a christocentric view point, and Christianity as an act of God is the only true religion. This is Barth's position, and as a student of Barth's, this is van Buren's position, too. Obviously this leaves no room for Judaism (or any other religion for that matter). Van Buren continues the church's anti-Judaic tradition.

When van Buren leaves the University of Basel and returns to the United States, he feels a need to shake off his Barthian influence. God-talk is seen as impossible, and the belief that God acts in the world and in human lives is seen as unreal. We might understand van Buren to be returning to the discipline of 19th century Liberal Theology---the very thing that Barth was reacting against---in the sense that that discipline too has its starting point in the human and not with God. The problem with such a starting point, of course, and van Buren is a good example of this, is that one does say a lot about human beings, but one ends up never saying anything about God.

In both *The Secular Meaning of the Gospel* and *The Edges of Language* one can understand what van Buren is doing as that of trying to give meaning to the language of Christianity, where that language is understood to involve humans in a human world; secular Christianity is a this-world Christianity. If a use for "God" was found in *The Edges of Language* (no use for the word was found in *The Secular Meaning of the Gospel*), still the use was not that of referring. Rather, its use was to say something about the users of the language, namely, that they had reached the limit of what they could meaningfully say, in their longing and desire to say all that they possibly could say about their Christian faith. This interprets a feature of religious language that was lacking in *The Secular Meaning of the Gospel*, namely, the feature of mystery, wonder, and awe. In this sense the theory of religious language that van Buren presents in *The Edges of Language* can be seen as a development of the theory he began in *The Secular Meaning of the Gospel.* In *The Secular Meaning of the Gospel* Christian language was understood to be expressing a "blik," a certain orientation towards life, a commitment to the Christian way of life, an intent to behave in a certain way. The Christian "blik" expresses an attitude, a morality, it is noncognitive language. Along with a certain "blik," the Christian also entertains a certain story, the story of Jesus. The story functions in two ways: (1) it constantly supports the "blik" of the believer, and (2) it can, and for some it does, cause the Christian "blik" to be acquired.

Jesus is the definitive free person for Christians. He was free from self and free for others. On Easter his disciples and then others who heard the Gospel (the story of Jesus) began to share in the freedom Jesus had; on Easter Jesus' freedom became contagious. For Christians salvation is freedom in the world, and it is the Christian hope that some day the whole world will be free as Jesus was free. This is the secular meaning of the Gospel.

The secular meaning of the Gospel is about human beings and this world; its concern is with historical reality. God is not to be found in this reality, and when the word "God" is spoken by believers, it is being used to say something about themselves and that which is of the greatest importance to them, namely, Jesus of Nazareth.

As we have already mentioned, van Buren under Barth's influence viewed Christianity as the only true religion. But this view changes as he attempts to shake off the Barthian influence. In *The Secular Meaning of the Gospel* and *The Edges of Language* van Buren's starting point is not the full revelation of God in Jesus Christ. Rather, the starting point is the human being, the human perspective, which van Buren views as world-bound, historical. From this starting point no religion, including Christianity, can be proven to be the only true one. All religions use exclusivistic language, but, for van Buren, this expresses the conviction with which a religious perspective is held; it does not express objective truth.

For van Buren, each religion will view another religion in terms of its own norm, not in terms of the norm of the religion being viewed. For example, Christianity will view another religion in terms of Jesus, not in terms of the norm of the religion it is viewing. In other words, for van Buren, each religion seems to be valid in terms of itself, but can only recognize the validity of other religions in terms of that which validates itself, and not in terms of the validity claimed by the other religion. This is certainly a move away from viewing Christianity as the only true religion. Christianity is seen as the universal norm of all religions, but it is so only for Christians. We do not see why van Buren did not make the further move of allowing each religion to acknowledge the validity of other religions based on the witnesses of the other religions. This would result in each religion no longer claiming superiority to all others, but rather, each claiming equal validity with all others. Still, van Buren does not make this move.

Van Buren's view of Judaism also changes during the period under review. He began simply continuing the church's tradition of anti-Judaism. In *The Secular Meaning of the Gospel* his "call" and "response" Christology was anti-Judaic. The christology of his secular Christianity was less susceptible to an anti-Judaic interpretation. In *The Edges of Language* van Buren shows signs that he is becoming interested in the Jewish-Christian dialogue. He defines Christians as having entered into Israel and as becoming Jews by adoption. Just exactly what this means must wait for van Buren's systematic view on the subject.

After *The Edges of Language* the entire focus of van Buren's work shifts. During the period which included *The Secular Meaning of the Gospel* and *The Edges of Language,* a period of perhaps twelve years, van Buren's focus is on attempting to give meaning to the language of Christianity, to answer the question: Can Christians give an account of the words they use? After *The Edges of Language* it is the Jewish-Christian dialogue that will consume his interest.

Chapter Two

Judaism's Attitude towards Christianity

We wish to set the stage for van Buren's work in the Jewish-Christian dialogue by outlining how Judaism has viewed Christianity and how Christianity has viewed Judaism before the dialogue, and by giving some sense of the dialogue leading up to van Buren. In this chapter we view the matter from the Jewish side. In the next chapter, Chapter Three, we view the matter from the Christian side. In our view, the dialogue actually gets started in the 20th century with the work of Franz Rosenzweig. We consider his contribution. In our attempt at gaining some sense of the dialogue from the Jewish side, we also consider the views of Martin Buber and Han Joachim Schoeps.

1. Before the Dialogue.

During the Talmudic Age (Alon 1989, 3) and particularly during the period 135-425 C.E., Judaism was involved in worldwide missionary activity in active competition — often successful — with

Christianity.[1] Not unlike Christianity then, we first must understand
Judaism's attitude towards the other, i.e. the non-Jew, as that of
potential convert. Indeed, at least one rabbi (Rabbi Simon ben Eleazar)
understood the Exile (Galuth) or dispersion of Israel of his own day
(occasioned by the Jewish wars, 66-70 C.E., with the accompanying
fall of Jerusalem and the destruction of the Temple, and the Bar
Kokhba revolt, 132-35 C.E.) as for the purpose of proselytizing: "The
Holy One, blessed be He, did not exile Israel among the nations for any
other reason than that proselytes should be added to them" (Pesachim
87b, as cited in Cohen 1978, 64).

However, the aggressive nature of Jewish proselytizing ended with
the Talmudic Age. Christianity's becoming the official religion of the
Roman Empire and the subsequent legislation against Jewish
proselytizing no doubt had a lot to do with this.[2] Still, in spite of
prohibition of proselytization, it continued in the Jewish community
into the Middle Ages, diminishing only towards the end of the period,
until finally Mendelssohn in the 18th century could say with the
support of the rabbinical authorities of his own time that Judaism was a
religion with no missionary tendencies (Katz 1961, 173).

While for Christianity the other, i.e. the non-Christian, could only
be viewed as a potential convert — there was no other way to regard
the other, at least in a positive way — the same is not true for Judaism.
Rabbinic Judaism does give some positive status to the non-Jew
beyond that of potential convert, albeit within the context of its own
faith system.

The subject of the status of the non-Jew or Gentile arises in the
rabbinic literature in discussions about who is to inherit "the world to
come," i.e. to whom belongs ultimate salvation:

> R. Eliezer declared,"No Gentiles will have a share in the World to
> Come; as it is said, 'The wicked shall return to the nether-world, even
> all the nations that forget God' (Psalm 9:17); 'the wicked' refers to the
> evil among Israel." R. Joshua said to him, "If the verse had stated 'The
> wicked shall return to the nether-world and all the nations,' and had
> stopped there, I should have agreed with you. Since, however, the text
> adds, 'that forget God,' behold, there must be righteous men among the
> nations who will have a share in the World to Come." (Tosefta
> Sanhedrin, as cited in Cohen 1978, 66)

According to Jacob Katz, this discussion continued and was never settled during the Talmudic period; voices on both sides of the issue continued to be heard (Katz 1961, 174). It was only with Maimonides in the twelfth century that the dispute is finally decided in favor of the view, "The righteous of all people have a part in the world to come" (Katz 1961, 174). The dispute ends in the sense that after Maimonides the opposing view is no longer heard; Maimonides' view becomes the official Jewish view. But now the question becomes: What does it mean to be a righteous Gentile, or, what is the criterion for the use of 'righteous' in righteous Gentile? It is probably also the case that it is only with Maimonides that we get an explicit and definitive answer to this question.[3]

According to the Hebrew Bible (Genesis 9:8ff), God made a covenant with Noah. The Rabbis gave to this covenant seven commandments, which are usually given as prohibitions against idolatry, blasphemy, murder, incest and adultery, theft, and eating flesh from a live animal; however, they also furnish a positive command to establish courts of justice, (for example, Genesis Rabbah, Noah, 24.8). The Rabbis taught that "the Nations of the World" i.e. the Gentiles, fall into the category of 'The sons of Noah,' and are bound by the covenant between God and Noah. Maimonides is perhaps the first to connect the Noachide laws clearly with the discussion about the ultimate salvation of the righteous Gentile, thereby making clear the basis on which a Gentile was to be accounted righteous: "Whoever professes to obey the seven Noachide laws and strives to keep them is classed with the devout among the Gentiles, and has a share in the world to come" (Mishnah Torah IV, Hilkot Melakim, Section X, Halakhah 2, as cited in Shoeps 1963, 14).

The word 'Christian' or 'Christianity' does not appear in the Talmud (Simon 1986, 179). Nevertheless, it is clear that both the Gentile church and Jewish Christianity are discussed there, as well as in other rabbinic literature of the Talmudic period.[4] It is also clear that for this period the church is classed with idolatry,[5] so that, even if Judaism does allow some religious validity to Gentiles as Gentiles — the righteous among them — Christians would be excluded from this group on the basis of their Christianity. We will see that the exact opposite of this is true of Judaism of the Middle Ages.

Maimonides also considered Christianity to be idolatrous, both for liturgical reasons---the church employed icons in its worship — and for more theological reasons — Maimonides took strong exception to Christian Trinitarianism.[6] Nevertheless, Maimonides goes beyond simply classifying the church with idolatry, giving to it (and Islam) a new and interesting role.

> But there is no power in man to apprehend the thoughts of the Creator of the world....Thus these words of Jesus of Nazareth and this Arab [Muhammed] who came after him were only to prepare the way for the Messiah-King and to order the whole world to serve the Lord altogether, as it says in Scripture, "For I shall unite all the peoples into a pure speech, all of them to call upon the name of the Lord and to serve Him with one shoulder.[7]

For Maimonides, the Messianic Age[8] is not a period which starts only after the end of history, a period that is beyond history, but rather, it is itself a part of the historical process. The Messiah-King is a political ruler who puts the Torah into full and universal practice. All the peoples of the world accept Judaism in the Messianic Age; and Christians (and Muslims) return to their true spiritual origins in Judaism, having fulfilled their role of preparing the non-Jews for the Messianic Age and the full acceptance of Judaism.[9]

This preparatory theory concerning Christianity (and Islam) in Maimonides is not shared by the Rabbis of the Middle Ages. For them Christians are simply included in the designation, "Nations of the World," and viewed as idolaters. In other words, both the way in which Christians are referred to and the way they are viewed is simply a continuation of the practice found in the Talmudic period. But this is true only on a doctrinal level. On a more practical level, where halahkic decisions had to be made concerning contact between Jews and Gentiles, particularly economic contact, Christians were gaining a status between that of idolater and Jew. Christians began to be viewed in terms of the Covenant with Noah and the seven Noachide laws. In the Talmudic period Gentiles were considered to be idolaters unless individually proven to be obeying the seven Noachide laws, while in the Middle Ages Christians collectively ,by virtue of their Christianity, were considered to be obeying the Noachide laws, and therefore not idolaters (Katz 1961, Chapter two).

The reason for this change in status of Christianity in European Jewry of the Middle Ages was the changed situation of the Jews themselves. In Talmudic times the Jews were relatively self-sufficient and could without undue hardship observe the Talmudic restrictions against contact with Gentiles, while in the European Middle Ages they were a small minority living in a wholly Christian society. Out of economic necessity many of the Talmudic restrictions against contact with Gentiles were not being observed. A way had to be found of rationalizing this non-observance if Jewish economic relations with Christians were to be justified by Jewish law (Katz 1961, Chapter three).

The way in which the non-idolatrous status of Christianity was established by the Rabbis of the Middle Ages was by the bracketing of the Christians of their own day from the idolaters of the Talmudic period. Perhaps the best example of this is R. Menahem Ha-Me'iri, who was active in Provence at the turn of the 14th century. R. Menahem Ha-Me'iri called his Christian contemporaries "nations restricted by the ways of religion," and those of Talmudic times "nations not delimited by the ways of religion." On the basis of this distinction between two kinds of Gentiles, R. Menahem Ha-Me'iri justified the non-observance of many segregative laws.[10]

Throughout the Middle Ages Judaism moves toward viewing Christianity in a positive way as the faith of others. It does so by adding to its negative claim that Christians are not idolaters, positive claims as well, claims such as that they (Jews and Christians) have a common tradition and worship the same God.[11] While the motivation for this change in attitude might have been pure expediency, Katz argues that this was not entirely true: "...a new evaluation of Christianity, as a non-idolatrous religion, was evincing itself" (Katz 1961, 163).

Moses Mendelssohn (18th century) goes far beyond what the Rabbis of the Middle Ages, or even the most progressive Rabbis of his own generation, would have said in terms of the relationship between Judaism and Christianity. Indeed, Mendelssohn represents a new type of Jew, the 'Enlightened' Jew, or Maskil.

For Mendelssohn, Judaism is a particular religion, which is to say it is only meant for the Jewish people. They have this religion by a special revelation of God, and are not to seek salvation by any other means. Still, this does not mean that the non-Jew is left without a means of salvation. For all the other peoples of the world salvation can be achieved by exercising reason in order to live in harmony with the Laws of Nature, which are both (reason and the Laws of Nature) innate in every human being. Indeed, the tenets of Judaism themselves, while revealed truth, could be discovered by reason alone (Katz 1961, 169-181).

On this view, all the peoples of the world are on the same footing in terms of religion and salvation. This is so because the view itself rests on the notion of a common humanity of all people. Theoretically, then, it is possible that the religions of all peoples might be equally valid. Whether in fact this is true is determined by an evaluation as to their reasonableness, i.e. how rational they are. When Mendelssohn was forced against his will, or at least against his own preference, to defend Judaism against the claims of Christianity, his stand was not different from his predecessors in their polemics. In terms of his own view, Judaism was superior to Christianity because it was more rational (Katz 1961, 171).

It was not Mendelssohn's purpose to position Judaism to dialogue with Christianity. He championed tolerance. For him it would seem religion is best seen as a private matter, private, that is, to the community that shares a particular religion. But this will not do when it comes to Christianity and Judaism. This is so mainly because Christianity, as we shall see, includes Judaism as part of its own self-definition. If the view of Judaism found within Christianity is to change, as we shall see the Christian participants in the Jewish-Christian dialogue feel it must, then this is best done in dialogue with Jews.

Still, we might ask if Mendelssohn's view might not be used as a way of starting a Jewish-Christian dialogue. The answer to this would seem to be, no. Mendelssohn is a product of the Rationalism of his day. But both Christianity and Judaism would probably reject the nature of religion as understood by Rationalism. Absent from Mendelssohn's view of religion, for example, is something that is perhaps basic to both Christianity and Judaism — namely, God, who is actively involved in creation for the benefit of God's people.

If there is some value of Mendelssohn for the development of the Jewish-Christian dialogue, perhaps it lies in this: Mendelssohn confronts both sides with their claims to exclusiveness. Obviously there could be no dialogue if either side claims (or both sides claim) to be the sole depository of religious truth:

> Since the Creator intended all men for eternal bliss, an exclusive religion cannot be the true one. I venture to state this as a criterion for truth in religious matters. No revelation purporting to be alone capable

of saving men can be the true revelation, for it does not harmonize with the purposes of the all-merciful Creator (Shoeps 1963 , 103).

If with Mendelssohn's view we have not found Judaism postured to dialogue with Christianity, it should be equally clear that the Judaism preceding Mendelssohn did not have that posture either. During the Talmudic period both Christianity and Judaism denied the other's right even to exist. The posture was one of disputation. From the Jewish side Christians were seen as idolaters. While on a doctrinal level the disputation continued throughout the Middle Ages, still there was some interesting movement on the Jewish side. Nevertheless, this movement did not develop to the point of a dialogue posture. Christians would not have accepted the way they were variously characterized. Christianity's own witness was not accepted as a basis for discussing its own claim to be the recipient of revelation. This is clear of the preparatory theory of Maimonides and the various forms that that theory took in the 19th and 20th centuries (see page 171n9); and, this is equally clear of the classifying of Christians as 'the Sons of Noah' subject to the seven Noachide commandments. But, even if Katz is correct that Judaism of the Middle Ages was moving towards a positive evaluation of Christianity, it was not the case that the Rabbis of the period went so far as to acknowledge the validity of Christianity based on the Christian witness to itself. For this to happen we must move to the 20th century, where both Christians and Jews posture themselves for dialogue with one another and where the Jewish-Christian dialogue actually begins.

2. The Jewish-Christian Dialogue from the Jewish side.

Instead of surveying the Jewish-Christian dialogue, we shall select, first on the Jewish side, three representative participants. We do this because it is our purpose to neither attempt to assess where the dialogue itself is, nor the direction in which it is heading — this would be a work in itself — but simply to give some indication as to what it is about. We begin with Franz Rosenzweig.

2.1 Franz Rosenzweig.

Rosenzweig goes farther than any Jew before him in recognizing Christianity. He affirms the divine origin of Christianity, and this represents something basically novel for Judaism. Rosenzweig expresses his views in two formats: in dialogue with Christian friends,[12] constituting perhaps the first actual Jewish-Christian dialogue, and in his systematic theological treatise, *The Star of Redemption* (Rosenzweig 1985). In our attempt to present Rosenzweig's views on Christianity and Judaism, the interesting and novel way in which he sees their relationship, as well as the dynamics underlying both, we shall mainly be relying on *The Star of Redemption*.

A six-pointed star as a geometric image, and a star as astronomic image of a body that burns continuously at its core and sends out rays from its surface, are the two images around which Rosenzweig formulates his theological view of things. In presenting Rosenzweig's view we must begin with the star as a geometric image.

The geometric six-pointed star is actually two interconnected equilateral triangles. The top triangle represents the Protocosmos, and the bottom triangle represents the Cosmos. God, Man (using Rosenzweig's terminology), and World are the points of the top triangle, and Creation, Revelation, and Redemption are the points of the bottom one. God is the top point, and the opposite point is Redemption; opposite Man is Revelation, and opposite Creation is World.

God, Man, and World are the three elements of reality. But they only become reality when they are linked together by Creation, Revelation, and Redemption. Rosenzweig refers to the status of the three elements before linkage with Creation, Revelation, and Redemption in at least two ways: (1) In terms of the World, its status before Creation is that of being. After Creation its status is being-in-existence (Rosenzweig 1985, 131-32). He also says that the being of the World before Creation is its pre-existence (Rosenzweig 1985, 131). In other words, if you restrict the use of the word 'existence' to something after Creation, and yet you posit something before Creation, i.e. before it exists, you need to give it some status in order to speak of it at all. Rosenzweig says it has being. (2) But he also speaks of the three elements of reality in terms of existence/real existence. He speaks of the elements as having existence before the linkage and real existence after the linkage; the World exists before Creation and has real existence after Creation (Rosenzweig 1985, 133).

Again, God, World, and Man are the three elements of reality, that only become real themselves when they are linked with Creation, Revelation, and Redemption. Before this linkage they are independent of one another. Each is an entity unto itself, not relating to one another; they are solitary selves (Rosenzweig 1985, 84).

Still, things do not remain this way. God emerges out of God's self in an act of creation. The effect this has on the World is that it is moved out of its self-containedness and unmovedness into existence, and it manifests itself as creature. In this, God's first act, God reveals God's self as a creator God and as a living God, as a God of life (Rosenzweig 1985, 157).

God's second act is revelation. In it God reveals God's love to Man. This has the effect of bringing Man out of itself and into the World. Revelation awakens the soul to love as it is loved and with the love by which it is loved, God's love. Indeed, the soul is given a commandment to love: Love thy neighbor (Rosenzweig 1985, 214-15).

God's final act is that of redemption, world redemption. But, while world redemption is an act of God, God will only act in this way when God is entreated to do so by the whole world in prayer (Rosenzweig 1985, 288).

Prayer is a gift of God in revelation. Only when God reveals God's self to a soul in love is the soul able to pray. Prayer now becomes also an obligation, or at least one prayer is — prayer for God to complete what God has started, prayer for the redemption of the world (Rosenzweig 1985, 185 and 267).

God created and the world becomes; it becomes open to man. God reveals God's self to man in God's love, and man turns to the world in that same love. Each time man extends that love to his neighbor, that neighbor becomes a part of the world; the world gains part of a soul. When the soul of man as a whole experiences the love of God, then it becomes one soul, the world's soul; man and the world are united. When this happens, the world's soul goes up to God in prayer with the prayer of world redemption, and God then acts to redeem it; God can do no other (Rosenzweig 1985, 240 and 293).

Redemption is future, as creation is past, and revelation is present. Nevertheless, redemption's future is assured, it is inevitable; its future realization is redemption's destiny (Rosenzweig 1985, 224 and 226).

What happens to the world and to man in God's final act of redemption? They "disappear," they are "absorbed," "merged," "integrated" — all words used by Rosenzweig — into God (Rosenzweig 1985, 238, 258, and 260). Does this mean there is no personal after-life? It seems not. Each self becomes immortal; only now not in itself and not in the world, but in God (Rosenzweig 1985, 258 and 286).

God's final act is redemption. But this final action turns out to be not world redemption, but God's redemption of God's self. What remains with redemption is God; God becomes the One and All (Rosenzweig 1985, 238 and 258). The star collapses into a one that contains everything: "Only God becomes the unity that consummates everything." (Rosenzweig 1985, 258).

We are now ready to consider the star as an astronomical image in Rosenzweig's formulation of things. In this regard, the star is Judaism and Christianity. The two religions are the parts that make up the one star, the star of redemption. Judaism is the fiery core, Christianity the rays going forth from it.

> The fire burns at the core of the star...The fire of the core must burn incessantly. Its flame must eternally feed upon itself. It requires no fuel from without. Time has no power over it and must roll past. (Rosenzweig 1985, 298)

Judaism is independent and self-sustaining. But perhaps its greatest quality is that of being eternal. It has this quality by God's gift of the Torah (Rosenzweig 1985, 304). Still, what is emphasized about Judaism in Rosenzweig's presentation of it is the people, the eternal people, the people as rooted in itself, the people that sustains itself simply by giving birth to children. Jews are Jews by virtue of their birth; a Jew is born a Jew, or, as Rosensweig expresses it: "The natural propagation of the body guarantees it [the Jewish people] eternity" (Rosenzweig 1985, 299).

> The rays shoot forth from the fiery nucleus of the Star. They seek out a way through the long night of the times. (Rosenzweig 1985, 337)

Christianity is eternal too, but it is not the eternal people which exists outside of time. Its eternity is one of the way, the eternal path that exists in time. A path that must lead throughout the world, because it propagates itself not by birth but by Baptism. Christianity must proselytize; a Christian is made, not born.

For Rosenzweig, both Christianity and Judaism are revealed religions. The major holy days of both religions have corresponding significance: the festival of the deliverance from Egypt (the Exodus story) in Judaism corresponds to the Christmas season in Christianity; the festival of the revelation of the Ten Commandments (the giving of the Torah) corresponds to Easter. But here the correspondence seems to break off for Rosenzweig. There is nothing in Christianity corresponding to the Days of Awe, New Year's Day, and the Day of Atonement. On these days the Jewish people proleptically experience redemption. Christians on the other hand can experience only the beginning of redemption, which they do on the festival of Pentecost. It is here also that they begin their course into the world; they begin their course on the way to redemption. The reason the Jewish people can experience redemption in their worship, while Christians can experience only redemption's beginning in theirs, seems to go back to their basic natures as atemporal and temporal realities respectively. Judaism *is*, Christianity is becoming. Judaism is at the goal that Christianity is moving towards. Judaism can proleptically experience ultimate redemption, Christianity can experience the way of redemption, redemption already begun in Jesus Christ (Rosenzweig 1985, 365).

This view might seem like the preparatory theory, the view of Rabbi Judah Ha-Levi, Moses Maimonides and other Jewish thinkers who see Christianity as preparing the "Nations of the World" for the ultimate acceptance of Judaism, perhaps in the Messianic Age. But this would be a mistaken impression. For Rosenzweig, Judaism and Christianity are separate religions whose goal is not for the one to lead to the other, but rather for them both together, each in its own way, to bring redemption to the world; they exist for this purpose, and indeed, they need each other.

Judaism does not need Christianity in terms of its own life: "The fire is not aware of the rays, nor does it have need of their light for itself" (Rosenzweig 1985, 335). But Judaism does need Christianity in terms of God's plan for world redemption. By living an atemporal life within itself, Judaism has no contact with the world: "By anticipating redemption, the Jew purchases the possession of truth with the loss of the unredeemed world" (Rosenzweig 1985, 414). It is the role of Christianity to expand into the world for redemption's sake. In this sense, Judaism is the otherworldly religion, Christianity is the worldly one.

Christianity needs Judaism as its everpresent source; the rays cannot exist without the fiery core. And, again, this is in terms of redemption. Without Judaism, Christianity would lose its way. Without the everpresent reality of the Jews, the Bible would be a mere book which could easily fall victim to allegorical exegesis. The Christian message could become a purely spiritual one in which redemption is seen as already come, and in which the world seen as not spiritual is disposable. (Rosenzweig 1985, 414-15). Christianity could also lose its way by understanding its own expansion into the unredeemed world as expansion for its own sake, or for the sake of the church, rather than for the sake of world redemption (Rosenzweig 1985, 404).

Thus, Judaism and Christianity need each other, though in different ways. They both labor at the same task, world redemption, but in different ways. They both have part of the truth; neither has the whole truth (Rosenzweig 1985, 415-16). In terms of the star as an astronomical image, Judaism sees the light of the core, but not what the light illuminates, the world. Christianity does not see the light; its way is the rays that move into the world that the light illuminates. Nevertheless, though the two need each other for the common task given to both by God, still there is enmity between the two, an enmity for all time, which also according to Rosenzweig comes from God (Rosenzweig 1985, 415).

This enmity seems to be based again on the two natures of each — the one eternally there at the goal which the other is eternally moving towards. Christian hatred of the Jew is based on the fact that the Jewish people are a continual reminder to Christians that they have not reached the goal. But this hatred is really only self-hate projected onto the Jewish people, self-hate as a result of the Christian's own not-yet redeemedness (Rosenzweig 1985, 413).

Again, this enmity lasts until the End. It ends at the End because Judaism and Christianity end there, too. They disappear in the world day of the Lord.

> For not the way alone ends here, but life too. Eternal life, after all, endures only so long as life in general. There is eternal life only in contrast to the life of those who pave the eternal way...life too disappears. (Rosenzweig 1985, 380)

As we saw in considering Rosenzweig's image of the star as a geometrical image of the way things are, so here also in considering the star as an astronomical image of reality, we see that with redemption the star collapses into itself leaving neither Judaism nor Christianity nor indeed even a world, a redeemed world; but rather, God, God redeemed, God who has become the One and All (Rosenzweig 1985, 383).

In assessing the view of Rosenzweig for the Jewish-Christian dialogue, it is important to remember that the dialogue actually begins with him. Indeed, there are those who see the contemporary Jewish-Christian dialogue as inconceivable without its Jewish beginnings in Rosenzweig (Novak 1982, 74). The dialogue begins with Rosenzweig because he represents the first instance in which one side, the Jewish side, acknowledges the validity of the other side in terms that basically come from that other side. Nevertheless, this neither means that Christians would recognize themselves in Rosenzweig's characterization of them, at least not entirely, nor Jews perhaps in Rosenzweig's characterization of them.

There is a lack of equality between Christianity and Judaism in Rosenzweig's view. Christianity is basically dependent on Judaism, its life inferior. This fact seems due to the nature of the two religions. Judaism in its worship can experience the future redemption of the world because it is eternal, i.e. atemporal, while Christianity can at best experience the beginning of redemption because it exists in time. Judaism is at the goal that Christianity but seeks. It is hard to see how Christianity could accept the inequality of Judaism and Christianity found in Rosenzweig's view.

Rosenzweig wrote *The Star of Redemption* in 1919. It is questionable whether he would have characterized the Jewish people as atemporal and ahistorical if he had written his treatise after the Holocaust. He was opposed to the Zionist movement of his own day because it would have placed the people back in time, back in history, and would have rooted the people in something other than itself, in the Land or the nation. All of this of course would be opposed to Rosenzweig's understanding of his people as the eternal people. But would he have maintained this understanding if he had lived through the Holocaust and the founding of the state of Israel? Would Jews today accept Rosenzweig's characterization of Judaism as otherworldly or unworldly?

2.2 Martin Buber and Hans Joachim Schoeps.

In presenting the contribution to the Jewish-Christian dialogue of Martin Buber and Hans Joachim Schoeps our main concern will be to focus on how they overcome the difficulties we found in Rosenzweig's position, particularly with his treatment of Christianity vis-a-vis Judaism. As we shall see, they purchase equality for Christianity with Judaism, but at the price of any linkage existing between the two faiths.

Buber has been charged by some in the Jewish community with going too far in his assessment of Christianity in terms of its significance for Judaism, and a passage such as the following seems to lend support to this charge:

> From my youth onwards I have found in Jesus my great brother. That Christianity has regarded and does regard him as God and Savior has always appeared to me a fact of the highest importance which, for his sake and my own, I must endeavour to understand....I am more than ever certain that a great place belongs to him in Israel's history of faith and that this place cannot be described by any of the usual categories (Buber 1961, 12-13).

But in fact this passage will not support such a charge. The Jesus that Buber refers to in this passage is a Jesus that he attempts to present in the book from which this passage is taken, *Two Types of Faith*. This Jesus is not to be described using either the categories usually reserved for him by the Jewish community, e.g. messianic pretender, or by the categories of the Christian community. Buber's Jesus is totally within the context of Judaism. According to Buber, Jesus lived by faith as Emunah (trust), while the Christian lives by faith as Pistis, faith as a belief in a proposition (about Jesus).[13]

As we have mentioned before, a condition of dialogue is that both parties to the dialogue be willing to acknowledge each other based on each party's witness to itself. Certainly, Buber acknowledges the validity of Christianity. He says the following about Christianity in responding to some Christians witnessing to their faith:

> I see in all this a important testimony to the salvation which has come to the Gentiles through faith in Christ: they have found a God Who did not fail in times when their world collapsed, and further, One Who in

times when they found themselves under guilt granted atonement (Buber 1961, 132).

But more than acknowledging the validity of Christianity for Christians, something we understand Rosenzweig to have done before him, Buber seems also to understand that validity as equal to the validity of Judaism. They are both ways to God: "The gates of God stand open to all. The Christian need not go through Judaism, the Jew need not go through Christianity, in order to come to God" (Schoeps 1963, 158).

Buber expresses the validity of both religions in terms of mystery: Christianity and Judaism are both mysteries unto themselves with neither one able to perceive the mystery of the other, though each can acknowledge the other as mystery. They exist side by side, which is a further mystery, God's mystery.

> Every authentic sanctuary can acknowledge the mystery of every other authentic sanctuary. The mystery of the other one is internal to the latter and cannot be perceived from without. No one outside Israel can understand the mystery of Israel. And no one outside Christendom can understand the mystery of Christendom...How is it possible for the mysteries to exist side by side? That is God's mystery (Buber, as cited in Jacob 1961, 174).

We might wonder what the two sides would have to say to one another, given what Buber says here. Does Buber's position allow for dialogue at all? What we need to recognize is that Buber faces a Christianity that far from acknowledging Judaism, firmly believes in its nonvalidity. In other words, while Buber is attempting a dialogue posture, it is not — and Buber is aware that it is not — being recip-rocated. In spite of this Buber can say: "We can acknowledge as a mystery that which someone else confesses as the reality of his faith, though it opposes our own existence and is contrary to the knowledge of our own being" (Buber, as cited in Jacob 1961, 173).

For Buber, Christianity and Judaism are two equally valid religions; that is to say, as Judaism is valid for Jews, just so is Christianity valid for Christians. They are separate and distinct religious faiths, and they will remain so throughout history until the End when they are both gathered into the Kingdom of God.[14]

Hans Joachim Schoeps' view is similar to that of Buber. But Schoeps introduces convenantal language into the discussion, language that does not dominate the thinking of Rosenzweig or Buber, but, as we shall see, is important to many Christian thinkers wishing to make a contribution to the dialogue, including Paul M. van Buren. So, perhaps, it is important to consider a Jewish thinker who uses this language, too. Beyond this, Schoeps is worth considering because he is more explicit than Buber in drawing the relationship between Christianity and Judaism.

For Schoeps, Judaism and Christianity are both covenantal communities established by God. God established the Jewish community by the revelation upon Sinai, and established the Christian community by the revelation upon Golgotha. They represent two different covenants: Israel, the Eternal Covenant; Christianity, the New Covenant. The one is the way of salvation for the Jewish people, while the other is the way of salvation for Gentiles. The two religions are separate and distinct, moving through history parallel to each other. Schoeps places both religions in history and in time, moving towards a goal neither has reached. Still, they will come together, when both ways come to an end, when the goal is reached with the arrival of the Kingdom of God (Schoeps 1963, 4, 5, 6, 160).

Both Buber and Schoeps see Judaism and Christianity as equally valid religions. They acknowledge Christianity's validity for Gentiles as equal to Judaism's validity for Jews. They are both ways to God, both divine mysteries. In this way they overcome the difficulty with Rosenzweig's view that placed Christianity in a dependent and inferior position vis-a-vis Judaism. Still, the cost of this equality is the lack of any linkage between the two, any significant relationship between them. We may not be happy with the way Rosenzweig linked the two faiths; nevertheless, it seems that if we are to remain true to the history of Christianity and Judaism, we must link them in some way.

Rosenzweig, Buber, and Schoeps are representatives of the Jewish-Christian dialogue on the Jewish side because they acknowledged in some sense the validity of Christianity on Christianity's own terms, Buber and Schoeps perhaps going farther in this regard than Rosenzweig. As we have seen, Buber could even go so far as to acknowledge Christianity along with, or perhaps in spite of, its negative teaching about Judaism. It is not to be thought, however, that Christianity can itself come to a dialogue position with Judaism with its negative teaching about Judaism intact. But, as we shall see, this negative teaching is a part of Christianity's self-definition perhaps from the very beginning, certainly it was very early; and so it constitutes a special problem for any Christianity that would acknowledge and dialogue with Judaism. To map Christianity's attitude towards Judaism is to map its negative teaching about Judaism.

3. Summary.

Judaism and, as we shall see, Christianity both claimed the same thing for their validity; they both claimed to be the chosen people of God, i.e. Israel. They both denied that the other had a right to the claim. Consequently, for most of the history of their relationship, the two were disputants.

There was some movement in the way Judaism viewed Christianity up to the time of its dialogue posture in the 20th century. The movement was one of viewing Christianity in the beginning as idolatry, to viewing it (along with Islam) in a preparatory role to Judaism, to viewing Christianity in a positive way as a religion for others, i.e. non-Jews. Still, even with this latter movement, Judaism's view of Christianity was within its own witness and not in terms of Christianity's witness of itself.

It is only with Franz Rosenzweig that we begin to get a Jewish view that acknowledges Christianity on Christianity's own terms. Nevertheless, the way Rosenzweig subordinates Chrisitianity to Judaism and the inferiority of Christianity to Judaism in Rosenzweig's view are weaknesses that other Jewish participants to the dialogue have attempted to address. We considered the work of two such participants: Martin Buber and Hans Joachim Schoeps. Buber and Schoeps both attempt to redress the situation by viewing Judaism and Christianity as autonomous but equally valid religions. The greatest weakness with this view, especially from a Christian point of view, seems to be that it provides no linkage between the two faiths.

Chapter Three

Christianity's Attitude towards Judaism

Our task now is to give a sketch of the Christian attitude towards Judaism, its anti-Judaic tradition. After defining what we mean by anti-Judaism, we begin with Christian origins and the New Testament. The Christian attitude towards Judaism has been essentially negative and unchanging up to the 20th century when some Christians and some Churches[1] have repudiated Christianity's negative view of Judaism and have entered into the Jewish-Christian dialogue. To give a sense of this dialogue from the Christian perspective we have selected as representative the work of James Parkes, A. Roy Eckardt, and Rosemary Ruether.

1. Before the Dialogue: Christian Origins and the New Testament Period.

We must start by defining what we mean by anti-Judaism in terms of the New Testament. D.R.A. Hare has proposed a refinement within the category of Christian anti-Judaism as follows:

(a) Prophetic anti-Judaism, which is the sort of intra-Jewish critique characteristic of the biblical prophets and of later sectarian and reformist movements within Judaism.

(b) Jewish Christian anti-Judaism, which reflects the belief that God's decisive act with Israel is the death and resurrection of Jesus. In this view these events not only fulfil the promises of the old covenant but actually negate the primary characteristics of the covenant, namely, Temple, Torah, and ritual commandments. Faithful Gentiles now stand alongside faithful Jews as the "new" Israel. The path to repentance and redemption is still open for the "old" Israel, but only through faith in Jesus Christ.

(c) Gentilizing anti-Judaism, which emphasizes the newness of the "new" Israel, the Gentile character of Christianity, and God's final rejection of the "old" Israel (Hare 1979, 28-32).

First, we need to modify as well as comment upon Hare's definition. We agree with Gager (Gager 1983, 9) that the term "Prophetic anti-Judaism" is misleading in that it implies a negative attitude towards Judaism as such, although it is actually meant to describe an internal debate in which, though the meaning of symbols is in dispute, the validity of the symbols themselves is not. Therefore, we take Gager's suggestion and substitute 'intra-Jewish polemic' for 'Prophetic Anti-Judaism'. Also, the use of "new" Israel and "old" Israel needs to be used with caution. Peter Richardson has shown that Justin Martyr (in the middle of the second century, C.E.) was the first Christian writer to identify Christianity with Israel in explicit terms (Richardson 1969, 9-17 and 74). Such language is not found anywhere in the New Testament.[2] Of course one could argue that the notion behind this language can be found there, i.e. the notion is implicit in the New Testament. Nevertheless, caution is needed here.

In assessing the New Testament in terms of anti-Judaism we shall limit ourselves to the four Gospels and The Acts of the Apostles. Paul has traditionally been interpreted as having an anti-Judaic posture. Indeed the three thinkers that we have selected as representative of the Jewish-Christian dialogue on the Christian side interpret Paul in the traditional way, and therefore do not see him as helpful to the dialogue. But there has been a "reinventing" (Gager 1983, 97) of Paul in recent years, a paradigm shift in the interpretation of Paul's writing (Porter 1978-1979, 257-272). Indeed van Buren's position relies on Paul and the new interpretation of him.   Consequently, we shall put off considering Paul until we meet with him in the work of van Buren.

It would not be enough to assess the four Gospels and Acts in terms of anti-Judaism. They are somewhat removed from Jesus and Christian origins.   For example, the Gospel of Mark, which is generally understood to be the first Gospel written, is usually dated circa 70 C.E., perhaps some 40 years after the time of Jesus. If we were to assess Jesus at the narrative level of Mark to be anti-Judaic, we could not on the basis of this alone also judge Jesus to be anti-Judaic. At most we could say Mark's Jesus is anti-Judaic. But a burning question surely is: Does the Christian anti-Judaic tradition go back to Jesus himself? And so, we shall at least attempt to assess Jesus and Jesus traditions that pre-date the Gospels and Acts in terms of anti-Judaism.[3]

Unfortunately, "there is at the moment no firm consensus about Jesus, the nature of his activity, or the reasons for the groups that formed in his name and carried these [Jesus] traditions." (Mack 1988, 56). Nevertheless, there is incredible activity in Jesus research.[4] Our presentation of Jesus and the early Jesus groups will rely mainly but not entirely on the work of Burton L. Mack's book, *A Myth of Innocence*.   We recognize that other reconstructions of Christian beginnings are possible.

According to Mack, Jesus' audience was not specifically Jews, but Galileans, with Galilee of Jesus' time being a cultural mix of Jews and Hellenists, i.e. people of Greek culture.   Jesus' subject matter was contemporary life in Galilee, and his mode of addressing this subject was that of some world of wisdom thought.

Mack believes that Jesus would have been recognized in his own day on the model of the popular philosopher known as the Cynic. This is suggested both by the similarity in teaching and the similarity in lifestyles. As to lifestyles, the Cynics, or at least the not-so-famous ones, lived on the edges of society, begged for a living, and, as they wandered about from place to place, looked for opportunities to display the virtues of a life unencumbered by social conventions. They were a highly recognizable social phenomenon that was indicative of the time of Jesus, according to Mack. The instructions Jesus is said to have given his followers in the so-called "mission" speech in Q (Luke 10: 2-16) seems to describe Cynic practice:

> And he said to them, "The harvest is plentiful, but the laborers are few; pray therefore the Lord of the harvest to send out laborers into his harvest. Go your way; behold, I send you out as lambs in the midst of wolves. Carry no purse, no bag, no sandals; and salute no one on the road. Whatever house you enter, first say, 'Peace be to this house!' And if a son of peace is there, your peace shall rest upon him; but if not, it shall return to you. And remain in the same house, eating and drinking what they provide, for the laborer deserves his wages; do not go from house to house. Whenever you enter a town and they receive you, eat what is set before you; heal the sick in it and say to them, 'The kingdom of God has come near to you.' But whenever you enter a town and they do not receive you, go into its streets and say, 'Even the dust of your town that clings to our feet, we wipe off against you; nevertheless know this, that the kingdom of God has come near.' I tell you, it shall be more tolerable on that day for Sodom than for that town." (RSV Luke 10: 2-12)

The picture we get of Jesus from the earliest sources seems to be that of a wandering sage who advised his disciples to travel without staff — without a weapon — and without knapsack or purse to hold extra provisions and money. One was to live from handouts in exchange for teaching and healing. Again, the similarity of this picture of Jesus to Cynic practice of the time is striking.

As to teaching, Jesus' use of parables, aphorisms, and clever rejoinders is similar to the Cynic's way with words, according to Mack. Also, the themes found in these forms are in many cases familiar Cynic themes. According to Mack, the pronouncement story in Mark 2:15-17, for example, has the structure of a Cynic chreia (anecdote), and the saying about Jesus' family (Mark 3:33), the play on *patris* in the saying about the prophet's honor (Mark 6:4), the scatological humor in Mark 7:15, the image of the dogs and crumbs (Mark 7:28), and the evasion of well-wishers in Mark 1:38, all have themes that were traditional with Cynics (Mack 1988, 182-3).

Nevertheless, the Cynic model cannot explain two important things: (1) the emphasis upon God as the ruler of the kingdom (Kingdom of God) in Jesus' teaching, and (2) the fact that those who heard Jesus formed groups, all of which understood themselves to be religious movements with claims upon Jewish traditions. Consequently, Mack sees Jesus as having concerns with Jewish ethical and theocratic ideals. In other words, Mack feels it is necessary to use both Jewish and Hellenistic categories in order to understand Jesus correctly. He understands Jesus to be doing what the authors of Ben Sira and Wisdom of Solomon were doing, namely, combining Jewish and Hellenistic traditions of wisdom in order to make critical judgments about the times and to propose a religious ethic held to be in keeping with Jewish ideals. The difference between them and Jesus is that Jesus worked at a less literary level of life and thought (Mack 1988, 63-74).

According to Mack, Jesus took no polemical stance against specific institutions, Jewish or otherwise. His social criticism did not name those at fault, nor did he support an alternative program in light of his views as to what was wrong. He proposed no political program and did not organize a church (Mack 1988, 64). According to Mack, Jesus was a peasant with a sense for the precariousness of existence, who lived simply on the margins of society and invited others to share his view, a view that seems to have been organized around the notion of the kingdom of God (Mack 1988, 64 and 73).

We do not find in Jesus as Mack paints him any of the elements of Christian anti-Judaism. Jesus was a sage living in a culturally mixed Galilee, and used elements of that cultural mix to express Jewish concerns. Given this picture of Jesus, the amazing thing perhaps is that those who heard him formed groups in his name, Jesus groups representing the Jesus traditions.

There were many Jesus groups. The Pillars in Jerusalem, the Family of Jesus, the Congregation of Israel, the Synagogue reform movement, the Q community, and the Christ cult are perhaps just some of them; the ones of which there is some evidence. We do not have enough information about some groups to make an assessment in terms of anti-Judaism; perhaps this is true of the Family of Jesus. The evidence for the Christ cult is mainly the letters of Paul, and we have decided to assess Paul when we get to van Buren's treatment of him. At any rate, we have chosen to attempt to assess the Q community, and what Mack calls the Congregation of Israel, and the Synagogue reform movement.

Q (from Quelle meaning source) is a hypothetical document reconstructed from the Gospel of Matthew and the Gospel of Luke. We find no element of anti-Judaism in first edition Q.[5] It is mainly instructional and hortatory in character and addressed to the Q community, which was a Torah observant (except perhaps with some lacks in the food laws, Q10:8) Jewish-Christian group. Jesus seems to be depicted simply as a teacher or master, while also serving as a model to be imitated. Easter is not a part of this document. The death of Jesus is simply part of a "prophet's" vocation; there is no interest beyond that. If there were Gentiles in the first edition Q community, they were probably circumcised and required to be Torah observant. In any event, first edition Q saw no full-blown Gentile mission.

The story is different with second edition Q. The whole focus shifts to a polemic against "this generation," i.e. Israel. The reason for this seems to be the Q community's lack of success in converting Jews. In other words, Jews have not responded to the preaching of the Q community. Consequently, Q turns to a full-blown Gentile mission, and seems to understand Gentile participation in the Kingdom to be as a result of Israel's refusal (Kloppenborg, 1987, 236-7). In second edition Q, Jesus is depicted in exclusive ways: he is the sole mediator of divine knowledge, Q10:21-22; confession of Jesus is the definitive measure of salvation, Q12:8-9. For second edition Q, Jesus seems to be not just a herald of the Kingdom, but the final and definitive herald, Q7:1-10; Q11:14-23 (Kloppenborg 1987, 200).

It must be our judgment then that second edition Q has some of the elements of Jewish Christian anti-Judaism. But it does not have all of them. We find no anti-Temple polemic in Q, nor an abrogation of Torah and ritual commandments. Consequently, while there is clear movement towards a position of Jewish Christian anti-Judaism in second edition Q, it is our judgment that it does not really arrive at that position.

It is our judgment that the Congregation of Israel lacks any element of anti-Judaism. It is an early Jesus movement standing behind a collection of miracle stories used to compose the Gospels of Mark and John. It is a new society with Jesus as its founder, and understands itself using as model the epic tradition of Israel. The miracle stories which replicate in miniature the story of the Exodus from the crossing of the sea to the formation of the congregation in the wilderness, function for the group as its myth of origins. It is a mixed group (Jews and Gentiles) which would be considered "unclean" people from a Jewish point of view. Indeed, the group was not formed by attention to Jewish rituals; rather it is Jesus who heals and cleanses them without regard to the laws of purity. Nevertheless, there is no polemic against the "old" Israel. The group does not understand itself as a renewed or restored Israel, whereby the "old" Israel would be emptied of its validity; rather, without any claim to membership in Israel, it never-theless considers itself included (Mack 1988, 92-93, 222-224).

We likewise do not find any anti-Judaic elements in the Synagogue Reform movement. This early Jesus group is behind some of the pronouncement stories in Mark's Gospel. It understood itself as a reform group within the synagogue. But not only did it fail to reform the synagogue in conformity with its own beliefs, it was thrown out of synagogue. This Jesus group was mixed, and its behavior was seen as unclean from a Pharisaic point of view. Indeed, the group came into conflict with the Pharisaic codes of obligation, ritual purity, and halakhah. Nevertheless, this does not indicate by itself any anti-Judaic attitude on the side of the Jesus group. The Judaism of this time is pluralistic, and the conflict is best seen as a family quarrel, both groups sharing the same sense of heritage and institutional context, the synagogue. Jesus seems to be depicted by this group as an authoritative teacher, there seems to be no interest in his death, and the crucifixion seems not to be significant (Mack 1988, 192-205).

If we can find no anti-Judaic elements in the Jesus people of the Synagogue Reform movement, still we can wonder how this group develops when it is thrown out of synagogue, and therefore no longer can understand itself in terms of that institution. Mack believes that the author of the Gospel of Mark was a member of this Jesus group and wrote his Gospel at least in part as an attempt to redefine the group's identity after it had lost its synagogue context.

Let us summarize briefly before moving on to an assessment of anti-Judaism in terms of the canonical Gospels and Acts of the Apostles. We have judged Jesus as he has been painted by Mack as lacking any of the elements of anti-Judaism. Our judgment is the same for the Jesus groups we have considered, except for the second edition Q community, which, while it could not be judged to be Jewish Christian anti-Judaic, still, because it had some of the elements of that position, we judged it to be approaching the position of Jewish Christian anti-Judaism.

While there may be elements of Christian anti-Judaism in some of the Jesus groups that pre-date the canonical Gospels, and therefore, there may have been a development in the direction of Christian anti-Judaism in some Jesus groups, nevertheless it is our opinion that Christian anti-Judaism itself is not met with until we reach the level of the Gospel narratives themselves. It is our judgment that the Gospel according to Mark has a position of Jewish Christian anti-Judaism. While Mark may indict every Jewish group he can bring to mind for rejecting Jesus, still he never makes that final move of indicting "the Jews," or Israel as such. In other words, Mark does not make a claim that would move his Gospel from the position of Jewish Christian anti-Judaism to the final position of Gentilizing anti-Judaism. The same is not true though for the other canonical Gospels. Matthew, Luke, and John, we feel, must be seen as having the position of Gentilizing anti-Judaism.

It is Matthew's position that Israel's rejection of the gospel proves Israel unworthy of it (Mtt. 22:8). God in turn rejects Israel and gives to the church what was once the exclusive privilege of Israel (Mtt. 21:43).[6] Hare argues that Mtt. 23:37-39 is to show that God is abandoning his people (Hare 1979, 39). With Israel rejected and the gospel the exclusive privilege of the church, its mission is directed now exclusively to the Gentile world, (Mtt. 28:19). Matthew's Gospel has all the elements of Gentilizing anti-Judaism.

It is perhaps more difficult to assess Luke-Acts in terms of anti-Judaism. Hare does not believe Luke-Acts has the position of Gentilizing anti-Judaism (Hare 1979, 35-38). Likewise Robert C. Tannehill does not believe Luke-Acts has the position of Gentilizing anti-Judaism. For Tannehill Luke never resolves the tension between the Christian message that says that Jesus Christ is the fulfillment of God's promise to Israel, and Israel's rejection of that message. Luke never resolves the theological problem as to how the Christian message can remain valid in the face of Jewish rejection. Instead Luke lets the tension stand, offering no solution except perhaps the patient and persistent preaching of the gospel in hope that the situation will change (Tannehill 1988, 88,101). Sanders in his study on the subject concludes that Luke-Acts has in our terminology the position of Gentilizing anti-Judaism. He argues that the true role of the Jewish people is prefigured in the Nazareth episode (Lk. 4:16-30), and that the Passion narrative, the martyrdom of Stephen, and finally the Pauline passion narrative, is but a becoming by stages what the Nazareth episode had already shown the role of the Jews to be; namely, that of being rejected by God because they had rejected God, and consequently, the taking of salvation to Gentiles and not to Jews (Sanders 1987, 83, 164-68).

Perhaps the Gentilizing anti-Judaic message of God's rejection of "the Jews" finds its peak, at least in the context of the New Testament, in the extended, increasingly bitter invectives hurled at "the Jews" by the Johannine Jesus:

> You are of your father the devil, and your will is to do your father's desires. He was a murderer from the beginning, and has nothing to do with the truth, because there is no truth in him. When he lies, he speaks according to his own nature, for he is a liar and the father of lies. But, because I tell the truth, you do not believe me. Jn.8:44-45. (RSV)

2. Before the Dialogue: Post-New Testament Period.

The essential elements of Christian anti-Judaism that can be found in the New Testament — Christological exposition, criticism of the Jewish law, especially the ritual law which has been abrogated under the new covenant, and proof that Israel has been rejected and the Gentiles called — continues and is further developed in the Adversus Judaeos writings of the Church Fathers. If there is a difference between the Christian anti-Judaism in the New Testament and that of the Church Fathers, it is perhaps this: What is implicit in the New Testament, and therefore requires a good deal of interpretation to uncover, is explicit in the Church Fathers. Also, the kind of invectives hurled at "the Jews" that can be found in some New Testament material, especially the Gospel of John, pales in comparison to that found in some of the Church Fathers, especially the sermons of John Chrysostom.[7]

The church's negative teaching about Judaism, particularly that it was no longer valid, being superseded by the church, and indeed that it had ended with the coming of Christ, was contradicted by reality. Judaism in fact did not end with the founding of the church. Indeed, Judaism continued, and, as we have had occasion to mention already, was a major religion with worldwide missionary activity and in active competition with Christianity until the time that the church became the official religion of the Roman Empire. This glaring contradiction between church teaching about Judaism and the reality of Judaism was a problem for the church, a problem left for Augustine to solve. He solved it this way: It is the will and plan of God that the Diaspora of the Jews was to continue to exist as a negative witness to Christianity, a witness as to what happens to those who reject Christ (Augustine 1975, 28-32).

In a sense Augustine's solution is the culmination of a theme that has its beginnings in the New Testament. God has rejected the Jews because the Jews rejected the gospel by their own rejection, including the killing, of Christ. Luke and Matthew clearly go beyond Mark in laying responsibility for Jesus' death upon the entire Jewish people; where Mark has "the crowd" (Mk. 15:8,11,15), Luke substitutes "the people" (Lk. 23:13), and Matthew "all the people" (Mtt. 27:25). Indeed, in Luke and John Jews, not Romans, do the actual killing. In Acts the theme that Israel as a whole is responsible for Jesus' death receives repeated mention (Acts 2:36; 3:13,15; 13:27f). Consequently, not only has God rejected the Jewish people; God is angry with them as well. Mtt. 22:7 ("The king was angry, and he sent his troops and destroyed those murderers and burned their city.") is a Matthean insertion into the Marriage Feast (Mtt. 22:1-11), which Matthew got from Q (compare Lk. 14:16-24). The destruction of Jerusalem in 70 C.E. is here presented as the punishment inflicted on Israel by God because of the rejection of the gospel and persecution of its missionaries. Perhaps Justin Martyr (100-165 C.E.) in his *Dialogue with Trypho the Jew* is the first to claim that Jews suffer because they killed Christ:

> For the circumcision according to the flesh, which is from Abraham, was given for a sign that you may be separated from other nations, and from us, and that you alone may suffer that which you now justly suffer; and that your land may be desolate, and your cities burned with fire; and that strangers may eat your fruit in your presence, and not one of you may go up to Jerusalem. Accordingly these things have happened to you in fairness and justice...for you have slain the Just One...[8]

If Justin Martyr is the first Christian writer to claim that the bad things that happen to the Jewish people are God's punishment of them because they killed Christ, he is not the last; it becomes a commonplace in the Church Fathers.[9]

The suffering that Justin Martyr is referring to in the above passage is that resulting from the Jewish wars of 66-70 C.E. and the Bar Kokhba revolt under Hadrian in 132-5 C.E. It is in these events that Israel, beside losing the Temple and being expelled from Jerusalem, also loses its status as a State. Thus the long period of the diaspora of the Jews begins. And, again, it is Augustine in his attempt to explain the continued existence of the Jewish people (Judaism) in spite of church teaching to the contrary, who presents the view that the diaspora-status of the Jews is a permanent status willed by God as a negative witness to the church and to Christ. The myth of the wandering Jew, desolate and homeless, is born; a myth which guides the church in its relationship to the Jewish people throughout the Middle Ages. Also, once Christianity becomes the official religion of the Roman Empire, the church makes sure there is legislation that guarantees that the actual situation of the Jewish people corresponds to the church's teaching about them.[10]

The church's negative teaching about Judaism, which as we have seen has its foundation in the New Testament itself, has been a fixed part of church teaching for most of its history. It does not matter which Christian thinker we survey, nor which Church; anti-Judaism is part of the theology expressed. Anti-Judaism is as much a part of the theology of Martin Luther and John Calvin, for example, as it is a part of the Church Fathers. Nevertheless, in this century there have been some Churches and some Christian thinkers who have attempted to remove anti-Judaism from Christian teaching and to do so in the context of the Jewish-Christian dialogue.

3. The Jewish-Christian Dialogue from the Christian side.

Many of those from the Christian side who have come to the dialogue have done so out of the belief that the Holocaust — the extermination of six million Jews — could not have happened without the church's theological negative teaching about Judaism, and its social expression in antisemitism. In other words, it is this event, the Holocaust, along with the recognition that church teaching about Judaism and Jews had a role to play in that event, that has caused some Christian thinkers to re-examine the church's anti-Judaic posture. This is certainly true for the three authors we have chosen in our attempt to give a sense of the Jewish-Christian dialogue from the Christian side.[11] Let us cite Parkes on the relationship between Christian anti-Judaism and the Holocaust:

> The peculiar character which distinguishes antisemitism from other hostilities and prejudices which Jews have encountered is that it is not

based on the actual conduct of Jews. It is entirely a non-Jewish creation. So long as we are dealing with action and reaction we encounter issues which could be paralleled in the story of any people. Behaviour may be anti-Jewish, as other behaviour is anti-British or anti-French. But in the case of the Jews alone do we encounter this extraordinary and persistent current of hatred and denigration which is independent of Jewish conduct, and to which I believe the worst antisemitism should be confined.

This hatred and denigration have a quite clear and precise historical origin. They arise from Christian preaching and teaching from the time of the bitter controversies of the first century in which the two religions separated from each other. From that time up to today there has been an unbroken line which culminates in the massacre in our own day of six million Jews. The fact that the action of Hitler and his henchman was not really motivated by Christian sentiments, the fact that mingled with the ashes of murdered Jews are the ashes of German soldiers who refused to obey orders when they found out what those orders were, the fact that churches protested and that Christians risked their lives to save Jews — all these facts come into the picture, but unhappily they do not invalidate the basic statement that antisemitism from the fist century to the twentieth is a Christian creation and a Christian responsibility, whatever secondary causes may come into the picture." (Parkes, as cited in Eckardt, 15)

3.1 James Parkes.

Perhaps James Parkes' value for the Jewish-Christian dialogue is in the fact that he was one of the first to draw attention to the systematic anti-Judaism of early Christian literature, to the origins of anti-Judaism in the conflict between "the Church and the Synagogue," and to the consequences for the Jewish people of anti-Judaism in later history. His importance is in this, perhaps, rather than in the way he re-envisions the theological relationship of the two religions.[12]

Let us attempt to summarize Parkes' view of the relationship between Judaism and Christianity. Parkes understands Christianity as having its human center in the human being as person, and Judaism as having its center in the human being as member of a society, nation, or State (Parkes 1969, 11). Now, Parkes argues, just as the individual as person and the society of which the person is a member are in tension, just so are Christianity (person) and Judaism (society, nation) in tension with one another (Parkes 1960, 130-31). From this Parkes concludes:

"Because the same man is both a person in himself and a member of a natural community, does he not need the insights of both Judaism and Christianity? ...The conclusion to which I find myself forced is the apparently absurd proposal that man needs both (Parkes 1969, 16)." In Rosenzweig we saw that Judaism and Christianity on one level at least were related as parts of a whole, both doing their part in God's plan for world redemption; both had part of the truth, neither was in possession of the whole truth. Parkes seems to envision Judaism and Christianity in a similar way — both are needed; together they make a whole. But for Parkes this relationship is not grounded in a divine plan or in God as in Rosenzweig, but in "man".

We do not believe that Parkes suggested re-envisioning of the relationship between Judaism and Christianity will advance the Jewish-Christian dialogue. Parkes seems to be saying that a Jew should look to Christianity to gain insight as to what it is to be a person, and a Christian needs to look to the Jewish community in order to gain insight into what it means to live in community. But aren't both Judaism and Christianity drawn too narrowly here? Surely there is a social dimension to Christianity, just as much as there is an individual dimension to Judaism; and this is true even if historically, as Parkes maintains, Christianity has emphasized the person, and Judaism "the people."

3.2. A. Roy Eckardt.

A. Roy Eckardt is one of the most prolific contributors to the Jewish-Christian dialogue. It is not to our purpose to attempt to evaluate his overall contribution to the dialogue (which we feel is enormous), but rather to simply present, as we did in the case of Parkes, Eckardt's view as to how Judaism and Christianity should be seen to relate to one another. Eckardt's view has been called a single-covenant view. Indeed, for Eckardt covenantal theology is what is used in order to explain his view on Judaism and Christianity, and how the two relate.

For Eckardt the covenant that God established with Israel in the Exodus-Sinai event is eternal; God is faithful to God's people, Israel (Echardt 1967, 41, 103). Torah was given to the people in the context of the covenant as the constitutive occasion of it. Torah observance then is the means by which the covenant is sustained on the people's side (Echardt 1967, 101).

But now the question becomes: What about the validity of Christianity? The church had taught that with the coming of Christ the validity that was once Israel's is now the church's. If that teaching is in error as Eckardt claims it is, (Echardt 1967, 141) so that the validity that was Israel's continues to be Israel's, then where is to be found the church's validity? Eckardt's answer to this question is this: God acted through Jesus Christ to bring the Gentile world into the Covenant with Israel.[13]

For Eckardt Christianity is meant for the Gentile world, and Judaism for Jews. That the first Christians were Jews, Eckardt understands as a "bridge-community (Eckardt 1967, 138-9). Once the gospel had reached the Gentile world the bridge-community had served its purpose. To the question: Why was the gospel first preached to Jews? Eckardt's response is: To whom else could it have been addressed? The reason the majority of Jews rejected the gospel was because that was God's plan. The message had to be preached to Jews first, after all, it came from them. But it was not meant for them; thus their rejection of it. God had meant it for the Gentiles (Eckardt 1967, 137). Thus, the Gentiles too become party to the Covenant, participants in the election of Israel, "...enthusiastic newcomers to the household of Israel"(Eckardt 1967,140).

While Jews and Christians are party to a single, unfolding covenant, Eckardt understands the two religious communities to have different functions. His views on this are much the same as those of Rosenzweig:

> One way is to emphasize that Judaism faces inward to the Jewish people while Christianity faces outward to the Gentiles. A second is to say that the Jewish role is one of "being" while the Christian role is one of "doing." A third is to affirm that the Jew fulfills his vocational call-ing by "staying with God" while the Christian fulfills his calling by "going out" into the world." (Eckardt 1967, 145)

Indeed, Eckardt believes what he is doing on the Christian side is what Rosenzweig has already done on the Jewish side:

> A Christian theology of the Jewish-Christian relationship is called to proclaim from the Christian side what Franz Rosenzweig has expressed

from the Jewish side: Judaism is the "star of redemption," Christianity the rays of the star." (Eckardt 1967, 151)

Still we do not think Eckardt would endorse Rosenzweig's understanding of Christianity as subordinate and inferior to Judaism, though he never addresses the issue. Eckardt does claim that Judaism is not subordinate to Christianity (Eckardt 1967, 151). Presumably the reverse is also true. We might infer because Judaism and Christianity belong to the one covenant for Eckardt, that he understands the two faiths to be equally valid. The difference between Eckardt and Rosenzweig is that for Eckardt Christians are in the household of Israel, guest in the household of God. Rosenzweig would never say that. For Eckardt Jesus Christ is the door that gets Christians into the house of Israel, the means by which the Gentiles are included; for Rosenzweig he is the wall, the wall of enmity, that keeps the two faith communities apart.

In *Elder and Younger Brother* (1967) Eckardt affirms that the church will not give up its incarnational Christology, and that this will continue to be a problem for the Jewish-Christian dialogue (Eckardt 1967, 159). But in *Jews and Christians* (1986) he claims that incarnationism is false (Eckardt 1986, 153), and that what is required of any post-Shoah Christian theology is a christology different from that of incarnationism (Eckardt 1986, 144-5). It remains a weakness of Eckardt's position that he does not provide us with such a christology.

Van Buren also holds to a single-covenant theory, and so, we shall hold off on our criticism of this approach until after we have presented van Buren's more systematic handling of the view. The strength of the single-covenant view is that it links the two faiths. The question is, does it do so in a way that would be acceptable to the two sides of the dialogue?

3.3 Rosemary Ruether

Rosemary Ruether represents a two covenant perspective on the relationship between Judaism and Christianity. We shall now attempt to do justice to this perspective as represented by her.

For Ruether Christian anti-Judaism is the "left hand" of classical christology.[14] For her christology is the key issue, and, while she does not provide us with a comprehensive reformulation without an anti-

Judaic "left hand," she does give us some indication how such a reformulation might go.

For Ruether the fundamental affirmation of Christian faith is the belief that Jesus is the Christ (Ruether 1979, 246), where 'Christ', the Greek translation of the Hebrew 'Messiah', has a purely Jewish meaning. In this sense the coming of the Messiah is inseparable from the coming of the Messianic Age. Now it is clear to both Jews and Christians that the Messianic Age has not arrived. So for the Jew this means that the Messiah has not come either. But then what sense can we make of the Christian claim that Jesus is the Messiah?

First, let us review how Ruether sees the church to have answered this question. Her position is that the church has "spiritualized the eschatological" and "historicized the eschatological," and that these are errors; errors in the sense that they do not remain faithful to the messianic idea.

Perhaps we need to begin by being clear on what is meant by the messianic idea. Here is what Ruether has to say about Messianism:

> Messianism has to do with that category which Christians talk about but have so little ability to grasp; namely, history; real visible history; endemic human sinfulness that still goes on long after "Christ has come"; wars, famines, unjust oppression; murder; the riddle of history and the human condition that goes on unresolved. Judaism alone among the human religions takes this seriously. Christianity, on the other hand, typically uses its christology to deny the question. Messianism has to do with the hope that someday this question will be resolved. This may be expressed crudely or naively or in the most ecstatic visions. But it has to do with setting history to rights, settling the score of unrequited evil. God intervenes, judges the good and the evil and makes appropriate retribution between them. God changes the human condition so that it sins no more. Evil vanishes and maybe even death. Creation reigns with God in fulfilled community. Things become "very good," as they were intended to be in the beginning. (Ruether 1979, 244)

Ruether has no quarrel with a soteriology that tries to mediate relation to the essence of God in some way that would transcend history and find a standpoint outside of it for personal salvation in an unredeemed world. Such a soteriology as this she calls Platonic soteriology. Where Ruether disagrees is where this soteriology would claim to be a christology that fulfills the Jewish messianic tradition. A soteriology that claims the messianic hope has already happened "spiritually" is the spiritualization of the eschatological, or better, the spiritualizing of the messianic. But this is illegitimate because the spiritualizing of the messianic is basically the denial of the messianic. Messianism does not lend itself to a spiritualizing interpretation; it is not about the salvation of souls in unredeemed times, it is about redemption of the times (Ruether 1979, 243-5).

The church has also historicized the eschatological. This means that the church placed the Messianic Age into history. It did this by declaring the absolute finality of the Christ event. All history "before Christ" is regarded as the era of "unredeemed man," with all those unresponsive to the Christian message remaining in this era, while Christian times take on the aura of messianic glory (Ruether 1979, 247).

The problem with this is that while absolute language might be appropriate to eschatological realities, it is not appropriate to historical reality. Indeed, the consequence of the church's attribution to its eschatological encounter with the Christ event, its historicizing of the eschatological, has been not only Christian antisemitism, according to Ruether, but also the patterns of totalitarianism and imperialism that appeared in Christendom (Ruether 1979, 248).

For Ruether the Christ event is not to be understood as some final event that restructured history; that Jesus is the Christ does not mean that. Rather, messianic Christology must understand the Christ event (the Jesus story) in eschatological terms as paradigmatic and proleptic in nature; it is in this way we are to understand the Christian claim that Jesus is the Christ. But it is only paradigmatic and proleptic for those for whom it has become so, i.e. Christians. It does not invalidate Judaism that has been caught up in a different paradigm, that of the Exodus event (Ruether 1979, 249).

We need to say something about what it means to say that the Jesus story is paradigmatic and proleptic. To say that the Jesus story is paradigmatic for Christians is to say that this story mediates encounters with God and reawakens messianic hope (Reuther 1979, 255). In terms of messianism then, the meaning of Jesus is the Christ is that Jesus' hope of the Messianic Age is carried forward in those who take up the paradigm (Ruether 1979, 259). In no sense has Jesus brought in the Messianic Age, what he has brought is messianic hope. Perhaps it can be stated this way: "Jesus is the Christ" is an eschatological statement said by Christians, a statement that points towards an indefinite future for its fulfillment. To say that the Jesus story is proleptic for Christians means that not only does the story as paradigm mediate messianic hope, it also mediates a foretaste of that hope's realization.[15]

But just as the Jesus story is the paradigm of salvation for Christians, so is the Exodus story the paradigm of salvation for Jews (Ruether 1979, 249, 256). The Jesus story does not supersede and fulfil that story, rather the Jesus story is simply another story; it reduplicated the Exodus story; the two parallel each other (Ruether 1979, 249, 256).

Ruether's view on how to relate Judaism and Christianity can be understood on the model of two covenants. But while there are advantages to this view — the independent salvific validity of both religions is one — still, there are weaknesses, too. The greatest weakness we see is that this model does not provide any linkage between Judaism and Christianity. They are two different religions, separate and independent of one another. But surely, at least on the Christian side, something more is needed in terms of relating the two than simply asserting the independent validity of both.

Certainly the messianic Christology hinted at by Ruether would not be anti-Judaic. After all, what it seems to do is simply plant in the Christian what is already to be found in the Jew, namely, the hope for the Messianic Age. Still, there is a need for a systematic formulation of such a christology. Indeed, once one admits the continued validity of Judaism, which is what Ruether and the other Christian participants in the Jewish-Christian dialogue desire to do, then a whole reformulation of Christian theology is called for, one that is not anti-Judaic. What would such a theology look like? Paul M. van Buren is the only one who has set for himself the task of answering this question thoroughly.

4. Summary.

For most of its history Christianity has been unmoving in its view of Judaism as having been displaced by Christianity. Indeed, its anti-Judaic tradition was seen as part of its self-affirmation and self-definition early in its beginning, having its roots in the New Testament itself. The effect of the church's anti-Judaic teaching, the social expression of which is antisemitism, has been devastating on the Jewish people. While there has been some criticism by Christians of the church's teaching about Judaism before the Holocaust, James

Parkes perhaps being the best example, the Christian participation in the Jewish-Christian dialogue is for the most part a post-Holocaust phenomenon. Which is to say, it is the belief that the church's anti-Judaic tradition had a role to play in the fact of the Holocaust that has brought many Christians to the Jewish-Christian dialogue.

To give a sense of the dialogue from the Christian side, we considered James Parkes, A. Roy Eckardt, and Rosemary Ruether. We focused on how the three envisioned a new relationship between Judaism and Christianity: Parkes' person/community model, the one covenant theory of Eckardt, and the two covenant theory of Ruether. We found reason to think that the person/community model would not be helpful to the dialogue. The two covenant theory of Ruether has its strengths, but it fails to provide any meaningful linkage between the two faiths, which would seem to be a necessity, at least from the Christian side — Christianity cannot help but refer to Judaism in its own self-definition. The one covenant view is a view also held by van Buren. So we have held off assessing such a view until considering van Buren's contribution to the dialogue. Van Buren is the only participant who has given a systematic view of Christianity that has repudiated its anti-Judaic past and has acknowledged the eternal covenant between God and Israel. What does Christianity as van Buren has envisioned it, look like? Would it be acceptable to Christians? Would it be acceptable to Jews? To answer these questions is the task before us.

Chapter Four

Van Buren's Methodology and an Argument for a Theology of the Jewish-Christian Reality

The purpose of this chapter is to present van Buren's method for developing "A Theology of the Jewish-Christian Reality." But, while doing this, we also discover an argument by van Buren for the necessity for a theology of the kind he wishes to develop. Van Buren's argument for the need for "A Theology of the Jewish-Christian Reality" is itself a unique contribution to the Jewish-Christian dialogue. In presenting van Buren's method we also discover a presupposition, his one covenant theory, which is itself only developed within the context of his theology. Van Buren's one covenant theory is the center piece of his theological picture of the Jewish-Christian reality.

1. The Starting Point.

Van Buren's theology of the Jewish-Christian reality is a Christian theology; van Buren is a Christian theologian. The starting point for any theology is for van Buren the church, (van Buren 1983, 71 and van Buren, 1980, 8) what he refers to as the Way in *Discerning the Way.*

"The Way" was an early designation of the church (Acts 9:2; 19:9,23; 22:4; 24:14,22). Van Buren chooses this way of referring to the church not so much because of this however, but rather because it suggests a certain feature of the church that is important to him, namely that it is an historical entity; "We are on a journey, a path through history: we are on a Way"(van Buren 1980, 5).

The reason that an historical entity is chosen as the starting point is because van Buren is committed to viewing reality as history (van Buren, 1980, 5, 8, and 22).[1] This is the same commitment that is found in *The Secular Meaning of the Gospel* and in *The Edges of Language*. A significant difference between the van Buren of that period however, and the van Buren of the period that concerns us now, the Jewish-Christian dialogue period, is that concerning God. In the earlier period there was no room for God in reality viewed as history. In this later period, as we shall see, van Buren is able to keep his commitment to viewing reality as history by introducing God into history; that is to say, by viewing God along with everything else within an historical framework; God too has a past, as well as a present and a future. Van Buren is as consistent in the period that concerns us now as he was in the earlier period in viewing everything in terms of history.

The reason that the church is chosen as the historical entity that is to be the starting point for a theology that wishes to make a contribution to the Jewish-Christian dialogue, is because such a contribution must come from a Christian perspective or from a Jewish one---there is no neutral or common ground on which to dialogue (van Buren 1980, 35) — and the person wishing to make a contribution, namely van Buren himself, happens to be a Christian.

If the starting point is the church but the church is an historical entity, then there is still the question, which church? Do we begin with the early church (the church's past), or the present or future church? At what point in history do we begin? For van Buren, the church exists in the present, looks to the future, and then retells the past (van Buren 1988, 10-18, and 204). The starting point for a theological task of whatever sort is the church of the present.

2. Van Buren's definition of theology.

In *Discerning the Way* van Buren, consistent with his metaphorical use of "the Way" as the church, describes as walkers the ones who find themselves in the Way (van Buren 1980, 17). He does this to emphasize that Christians are primarily defined by the way they move through history; how they live, behave, etc. But, because how and in what direction Christians are walking is a function of their understanding of who they are, (van Buren 1988, 21) while walking they also talk among themselves. In so far as the conversation is about the Way and their walking in it, in so far as the conversation is about the church and what it is doing, the direction in which it is going, it is a theological conversation:

> ...theology is and has always been, as I understand it, a contribution to — in the form of critical reflection on — a conversation in ipso itinere (while walking) among members of the Christian church concerning the Way on which they found themselves (van Buren 1980, 4).

In *The Secular Meaning of the Gospel* and in *The Edges of Language* van Buren had expanded the context in which theology was to be done to that of the culture of which he himself was a member. He now, in turning to the concerns of the Jewish-Christian dialogue, repudiates that context as the proper context for doing theology (van Buren 1980, 51-52), and returns to an understanding of theology's context which he inherited from Barth. Theology is the activity of the church, carried out within and on behalf of it (van Buren 1983, 37 and van *Buren, 1988, 20).*

If the contemporary church is the starting point for the theological enterprise viewed as a conversation within and for the church's benefit, the next question would seem to be, how does this conversation get started, and how does one determine the truth of the (theological) statements that one makes within this conversation? To answer this question is to understand how van Buren views the Bible and its use in the theological enterprise. Once again van Buren's basic commitment to reality as history comes into play.

3. Van Buren's approach to the Bible; its use for theology.

For van Buren, the Bible is the book that Christians carry that tells them of their beginnings and helps them get started in their walking and talking, helps them get started in their Christian lives and in their theological conversation (van Buren 1980, 120). He understands the content of the Bible this way:

> The content of this book, generally, is the story of the beginning of God's Way with His beloved creation into which we have been called to walk. It is therefore the beginning of our Way (van Buren, 1980, 130).

For van Buren, the Bible is history understood as the history of God with God's creation (van Buren 1980, 5 and 8).[2] The Bible is but the beginning of this story because while the Bible ends, the story the Bible tells does not end with the Bible, rather it continues to the present; the story the Bible tells, or rather begins, goes beyond the Bible and has not yet come to an end.

> The story, which opens with the Scriptures [the Hebrew Bible, the Tanakh] and continues in the Apostolic Writings [the New Testament] and the Talmud is not over. We find ourselves now somewhere in the middle of it (van Buren 1980, 144).

That the story continues but the Bible doesn't mean that the Bible cannot function as norm (Sola Scriptura) for theological statements;[3] such a function would be ahistorical and would not fit into van Buren's basic commitment of reality as history. What then is the norm for van Buren? In a way the norm is God. But not God per se, but rather God as God is discerned by his people (the church and the Jewish people) in the continuously unfolding story (van Buren 1983, 8-9).

The interesting way in which van Buren sees the need for a theology of the Jewish-Christian reality is by way of new revelation, "...discern[ing] the finger and voice of the Lord God of Israel in the postbiblical history" (van Buren 1983, 8-9). This in turn will lead to a new interpretation of the biblical story, and a new understanding of Christianity, a Christianity reflecting the Jewish-Christian reality.

Again, for van Buren history is the history of God with God's creation. The Bible tells the story of the beginning of this history and continues the story, but only up to a point: "The Bible is history-up-to-a-point"(van Buren 1980, 160). But if the story continues beyond the Bible's telling of it, how is one to discern it? Van Buren's answer is, new revelation. Indeed, such new revelation might move one to reinterpret the story from the very beginning, a story of the Jewish-Christian reality.

4. New Revelation.

Before presenting what van Buren believes might turn out to be new revelation and how this new revelation is to be recognized, we first should gain some understanding of what van Buren means by revelation.

For van Buren, revelation is an act of God towards people (van Buren 1980, 167). In this act God gives something, or at least the recipients of revelation perceive something to be given. Thus, revelation has a content; indeed, the Way as witnessed by those in the Way is a gift of God, the content of God's revelation (van Buren 1980, 2, 40).

Revelation has a pattern. It begins with an originating event; for van Buren this is the story of Abraham. The originating event constitutes tradition for those who make it their own. Individuals within the tradition may reinterpret the tradition based on historical events that are a part of their own lives. If such a reinterpretation is accepted by those holding the tradition, that is to say, if the reinterpretation of the received tradition itself becomes part of the tradition, then this (the reinterpretation) constitutes new revelation. We might describe van Buren's theory of revelation this way: Revelation is the reinterpretation of received tradition when such reinterpretation is, (1) based on recent events (recent to the reinterpretation) in Jewish history, and (2) accepted by the community that holds the tradition (van Buren 1980, 37-8, 166-71).

Van Buren's theory of revelation also suggests a method for doing theology — reinterpreting the Christian tradition based on recent historical events. Indeed, this will be van Buren's method for developing a Christian theology for the Jewish-Christian reality. He believes that he is continuing a method that produced the Bible itself:

> Redaction and canon criticism, which focus on the historical circumstances that gave shape to the individual books and their larger groupings, have helped us to see the Bible as consisting of layered reinterpretations of a sacred tradition occasioned by successive events in Israel's history. That structure is evidently open-ended. It invites further reinterpretation in response to further events, even up to our

own times, as it continually challenges our self-understanding and our reading of our own history (van Buren 1980, 6).

The reinterpretation of the Christian tradition, the development of which van Buren wishes to himself participate in, he finds in recent documents of the church. These are the same documents we referred to in Chapter Three.[4] These documents as we saw repudiate the church's anti-Judaic tradition and affirm the continued validity of the covenant between God and the Jewish people. Van Buren views this as a reinterpretation of the received tradition.

The historical events that occasioned the reinterpretation are the Holocaust and the establishment of the State of Israel (van Buren 1980, 176). It is interesting that van Buren does not put forth arguments that the Holocaust should be occasions for the church to re-think its anti-Judaic tradition; rather, he seems to rest content with simply making the observation that that is in fact what is happening (van Buren 1980, 177).

Van Buren is not claiming that there has in fact been new revelation. This is because he is well aware that, while there has been statements of the reinterpretation in important documents of the church, the church as a whole has not accepted these statements. And, by the criteria of van Buren's theory of revelation, only when this happens can one recognize these statements as new revelation.

Perhaps before this happens, the implication of a positive view of Judaism on Christianity needs to be worked out. This is the work van Buren sets for himself. It is not enough simply to repudiate the anti-Judaism of the church and to place in its stead an affirmation of the eternal covenant between God and the people Israel. This is so because, as we have seen, anti-Judaism functions for the church as a way of self-affirmation and self-definition. To repudiate anti-Judaism, one is left with the task of redefining Christianity. And, if such a redefinition, or what van Buren would call a reinterpretation of the Christian tradition, is to be recognized by the church as new revelation, then Christians are going to have to recognize themselves as characterized in this new revelation; Christians are going to have to accept the new definition of themselves. Whether they will is the test of, or the basis of the recognition of, the new revelation, including van Buren's theology of the Jewish-Christian reality.

Van Buren is aware that his theory of revelation is not complete. It is a theory of revelation as knowledge or understanding, while the result of revelation is primarily that of community (van Buren 1983, 23-4).

He introduced it for a specific purpose, namely, to argue that a re-evaluation of Christianity in terms of its view of Judaism is called for because of new revelation evident in documents of the church. Van Buren's argument for a reformulation of Christianity vis-a-vis Judaism by way of new revelation is a unique contribution to the Jewish-Christian dialogue by one of its Christian participants.

5. Summary.

We will need to elaborate on and evaluate van Buren's basic metaphysical commitments, what we might call his worldview. This we shall do at the appropriate place in our presentation of his theology of the Jewish-Christian reality. But we could not even get started in presenting van Buren's argument for the need for such a theology without at least mentioning one basic element within that worldview, namely that everything is viewed within an historical framework; van Buren is committed to viewing reality as history. We noted that this is a commitment that pre-dates his Jewish-Christian dialogue period, being a commitment first expressed in *The Secular Meaning of the Gospel.* If this commitment has not changed with van Buren's turning to the Jewish-Christian dialogue, nevertheless there has been an enormous reversal on van Buren's part. In the period that began with *The Secular Meaning of the Gospel* and ended with *The Edges of Language* van Buren claimed that God was not to be found in reality (history), while in his Jewish-Christian dialogue period he claims exactly that — God is to be found in reality (history). As we shall see, van Buren has an interesting doctrine of God.

The starting point for theology is the contemporary church viewed as an historical entity. Theology in turn is viewed as a task within the church for the benefit of the church; for the sake of its behavior and direction; for the sake of it finding its way through history. Here we note that van Buren returns to a Barthian understanding of the proper context and purpose of theology. In van Buren's secular period, the context of theology was culture, and its purpose seemed to be to make Christianity as much like culture as it could. From this broad context in van Buren's philosophy of religion period the context of theology is narrowed to that of the church in van Buren's Jewish-Christian dialogue period. This latter view of the proper context for theology is a view van Buren held early in his career under Barth. In some sense van Buren's Jewish-Christian dialogue period is a return to Barth.

The theological task begins with the Bible, but the Bible is itself not the norm for measuring the truth of theological statements. If Protestantism's norm is Sola Scriptura, and Roman Catholicism's norm is Scripture and tradition, van Buren's view is closer to that of the latter. Van Buren understands the danger of the church being its own norm, but he is forced to take this position because of his basic commitment of viewing reality as history. The Bible is essentially a story about God and God's people. But that story does not end with the Bible; it continues right up to the present. To discern the story in the present and to direct the story into the future (theology's task) might include for the church the need to recognize new revelation in its own day.

Van Buren contributes a theory of revelation. For him, the theological method is one of reinterpretation of the received tradition based on historical events involving the Jewish people. Such reinterpretation constitutes new revelation if it is acknowledged by the church; thus itself, if acknowledged, becoming part of church tradition.

Van Buren claims that indeed new revelation is emerging in our own day. It is evident in contemporary church documents that repudiate the church's anti-Judaic tradition while affirming the eternal covenant between God and the Jewish people. This reinterpretation of the received tradition is occasioned by the historical events of the Holocaust and the founding of the State of Israel.

Van Buren admits that this emerging new revelation has yet to be acknowledge by the church in general, and so may yet turn out not to be new revelation at all. Nevertheless, he wishes to participate in the development of this new revelation by reformulating Christianity vis-a-vis Judaism that the new revelation requires. The test of the value of van Buren's contribution will be in whether Christians can recognize themselves in van Buren's view of them, and therefore give approval to the reinterpretation of the tradition, give recognition to the new revelation.

This way of arguing for the need for Christianity's reformulation — in terms of new revelation and a theory of revelation that goes with it

— is a unique contribution by van Buren to the Jewish-Christian dialogue.

6. Further Methodological Concerns.

6.1 Van Buren's 'promise-confirmation' model.

As we have already indicated, van Buren's theological method for reformulating Christianity is to reinterpret the received tradition. Before turning to van Buren's theology of the Jewish-Christian reality, we should give more specificity to his method and recognize one of its presuppositions. In his reformulation van Buren begins with the Bible, indeed with the first book of the Bible, Genesis. We have already mentioned a number of things about van Buren's approach to the Bible. However, there are two further things we should consider in our endeavor to be more specific about van Buren's method. They are these: (1) van Buren's way of relating the church's Old Testament to its New Testament, and (2) his approach to the church's Old Testament. Van Buren interprets the Hebrew Bible, the church's Old Testament, by listening to the Jewish witness to that book. We need to know exactly what this means, and why van Buren believes this is the approach to take.

The church traditionally has viewed the Bible as composed of what it has called the Old Testament and the New Testament. It has viewed or understood the former in terms of the latter. Viewing the Bible the way van Buren does as a story, we might put it this way: The story that the Old Testament tells culminates in the story the New Testament tells; the story of Israel (Old Testament) culminates in the story of Jesus (New Testament). The church has also viewed the Bible as a whole as the story of Christ, seen as shadows and types in the Old Testament, while really and clearly only in the New Testament. In terms of relating the two main parts of its Bible, the church has often used the model of promise-fulfilment: What is promised in the Old Testament, namely the coming of Christ, is fulfilled in the New Testament. But, of course, all of these approaches are anti-Judaic. So the question becomes: How are Christians to understand the relationship between what the church has called the Old Testament and the New Testament, and what van Buren calls the Scriptures and the Apostolic Writings, when they have repudiated the church's anti-Judaic tradition and have acknowledged the eternal covenant between God and God's people, Israel?

Van Buren proposes what he calls a model of promise-confirmation: the Apostolic writings *confirm* the *promises* that God made to God's people, Israel (van Buren 1983, 30). Van Buren's favorite text for expressing this idea is 2 Cor. 1:20, "For all the promises of God find their Yes in [Christ Jesus]." The promise-fulfilment model would interpret the Yes here as confirmation as well, but would add that the promises of God referred to are all directed at the church and none at Israel. But, for van Buren, some of the promises of God are directed at Israel, and this verse confirms those promises. Van Buren gives as an example of a promise directed at Israel and not at the church that of God's promise of the Land. The church, in order to direct this promise at itself, spiritualized the promise.

A promise-confirmation model certainly addresses our question, but it does not say enough. If the Apostolic Writings confirm the promises made to Israel, obviously this is not all they do. According to van Buren, they also add their own message, namely that God through the Gospel is providing a way to include the Gentiles in God's covenant, and thereby, God is fulfilling a promise God made to Abraham (van Buren 1983, 87).

We will need to develop this very important point of van Buren's later. Our purpose for introducing it here is simply to show that van Buren himself uses a promise-fulfilment model in order to fully explain the relationship between the Hebrew Bible and the Apostolic Writings. Perhaps what is needed is a promise-confirmation-fulfilment model.

6.2 Van Buren's One-Covenant theory as a presupposition of his method.

In his reformulation of Christianity van Buren wishes to replace the church's anti-Judaic tradition with a more positive view of Judaism. This is really the only move one can make who wishes to repudiate the church's anti-Judaic tradition.. The only other possible move — replacing the anti-Judaic tradition with no view at all on Judaism — is not an option for the church. This is so because, as we have had occasion to mention previously, Christianity must refer to Judaism in order to make sense of itself. So now we have this question: How is

Christianity, that wishes to affirm the eternal covenant between God and Israel, to refer to Judaism?   What is called for is a positive approach. But how should Christians go about this task?

It seems one approach could be an historical one. One could argue that Christianity emerged out of Judaism, but that once it did emerge, it became an autonomous religion.   In other words, there is no theologically important relationship between the two religions. God did not intend for there to be anything other than two independent religious communities. Christians who would argue in this way might still wish to, and encourage the study of, Judaism from the Jewish sources. But here the motivation would be to try to undercut the image of the Jewish people and Judaism that the church's anti-Judaic tradition had produced. The motivation would not be to present Judaism as in some way theologically important for an understanding of Christianity in its on-going life today. Rather, the motivation would be to view in a positive way another religion that has salvific value distinct from but equal to that of Christianity. One might argue in this way. We believe Rosemary Ruether would argue like this. But this is not van Buren's approach.

Van Buren believes that the church needs a theology of the people Israel. Exactly what that theology is will have to wait until we consider his theology of the Jewish-Christian reality. But we cannot even get started on that task until we have some understanding of van Buren's method, why he proceeds in the way he does. We have said that his method for reformulating Christianity takes the form of a reinterpretation of the received tradition beginning with the Bible itself. Now we need to add this: In interpreting the Hebrew Bible van Buren listens to, and incorporates the witness of Israel. The witness of Israel means for van Buren the Talmud and other exegetical rabbinic litera-ture, as well as the work of other Jewish thinkers, both historical and contemporary; Franz Rosenzweig, Emil Fackenheim, and Irving Greenberg are examples of contemporary Jewish thinkers that van Buren listens to.

Van Buren's purpose in consulting Israel's witness to the texts which the church shares in common with Israel, is not simply to get Israel's help in forming a positive view of Judaism in and for itself. Van Buren argues that if the church acknowledges that Israel had something to say that the church needed to hear, namely what Israel said in the Scriptures, and acknowledges now the eternal covenant between God and Israel, then Israel continues to have something that the church needs to hear; the church has an obligation imposed by God to listen to the witness of Israel (van Buren 1983, 18-19). But there is something missing in this argument that only gets introduced and developed within the context of van Buren's theology of the Jewish-Christian reality itself, only gets introduced and developed while reinterpreting the Christian tradition that begins with the Bible. The missing element is van Buren's one covenant theory. The reason that the church must listen to the witness of Israel today, once it acknowledges the eternal covenant between God and God's people, is because the church is a part of that same covenant.

The same missing element we also find in an argument van Buren gives for his position that Israel is the fundamental context for doing christology:

> The fundamental context of the things concerning Jesus of Nazareth, according to the Apostolic witness was the covenant between God and Israel, and their continuing context is Israel in its continuing covenant with God. Israel and its story is therefore the fundamental context for developing a christology for the Jewish-Christian reality, or a christology for today. *(van Buren, 1988, 52)*

Our immediate task is to try to understand why we should agree with van Buren that Israel is the fundamental context for doing christology today. What we mean is this: We could agree with van Buren that the context in which the story about Jesus got started was the story of Israel. Indeed, this is all that van Buren establishes in the chapter in which the above quotation is taken. We could also agree with van Buren that the covenant between God and Israel is continuing. And, still, we would not have to concede to him that Israel is the fundamental context for doing christology today. We could argue that, while the church began as a sect within Judaism, it quickly moved out of Judaism and became an autonomous religion. The context for doing christology today is the church.

Something is missing in this statement by van Buren that would justify him in asserting Israel as the fundamental context for doing christology. We get a clue as to what it is that is missing in the following statement by van Buren:

Reflection on the place of christology, finally, raises the question of its context. There is no understanding without reference to the context of what is to be understood. The church's understanding of the things concerning Jesus of Nazareth is no exception: it will depend on the context in which the church sees them. Assuming the Jewish-Chrsitian reality as defined in *Discerning the Way* and *A Christian_Theology of the People Israel*, we shall have to consider the bearing of the context on the church's understanding of Christ. (van Buren 1988, 26)

With the above as a clue, it is our opinion that the missing item that justifies van Buren in asserting that Israel is the fundamental context in which christology is to be done, is his one covenant theory, which he develops in *A Christian Theology of the People Israel*. It is interesting that neither in the above quotation, nor in the chapter in which the fundamental basis of Israel as context for christology is asserted, does van Buren explicitly state that his one covenant theory is a condition of his contention. Nevertheless, it is our opinion that his one covenant theory is certainly presupposed. Otherwise we can find no reason for granting to van Buren anything more than that Israel *was* the context in which christology got started. In other words, we think that the reason van Buren understands Israel to be fundamental for doing christology is that christology is done in the context of covenant, and there is only one covenant. Christology cannot move out of the covenant in which it got started and of which Israel is the context because there is no place to move.

The method that van Buren uses — reinterpreting the Hebrew Bible based on listening to Israel's witness — presupposes the one covenant theory which van Buren develops within the context of his reinterpretation, within the context of his theology of the Jewish-Christian reality.

6.3 Summary.

Van Buren's method of reformulating Christianity vis-a-vis Judaism, based on the church's reversal of its position on Judaism from that of anti-Judaism to that of an acknowledgement of the eternal covenant between God and Israel, is to reinterpret the received tradition based on this reversal. For van Buren the method for doing the reformulation is this: One begins with the Bible; this is where Israel's story begins, this is where the church's story begins. One listens to

Israel's interpretation of its own text, the Hebrew Bible. For van Buren this means listening to Israel's witness found in rabbinic literature, as well as in the work of other Jewish authors including 20th century Jewish thinkers. Then one confirms what one hears and adds to it "a new chapter," beginning with the Apostolic Writings (the New Testament). Obviously, if the New Testament adds to and does not negate what is found in the Hebrew Bible, it will be interesting to see how van Buren deals with the anti-Judaic material which he himself acknowledges is to be found in the New Testament.

Finally, we have recognized that van Buren's method presupposes something which he only introduces and develops within the context of his theology of the Jewish-Christian reality itself, namely, his one covenant theory. As we shall see, this theory is at the heart of van Buren's theology of the Jewish-Christian reality. Van Buren's theology of the Jewish-Christian reality is a narrative theology; it tells a story. But it is also a covenantal theology; it tells a story of a covenant.

Chapter Five

A Theology of the Jewish-Christian Reality: Van Buren's Worldview

The purpose of this chapter is to introduce the worldview of van Buren's theology of the Jewish-Christian reality. By worldview we mean the basic structure and elements that make up reality. We might also understand van Buren's worldview as made up of commitments that van Buren cannot give up; they are ultimate (metaphysical) commitments.

1. The Creator and Creation.

Van Buren affirms the traditional doctrine of creatio ex nihilo: God created out of nothing everything that exists other than God God's self (van Buren 1983, 58). Nevertheless, what this act of Creation by God meant to God and creation is other than what one would find in traditional church teaching, i.e. in Western Christianity.

We can suppose that God existed in some sense before God's act of Creation, but this is not the God we know. The God we know is God our Creator[1]; God as God determined God's self to be by virtue of God's decision to become the Creator of heaven and earth, by virtue of

God freely willing to have an other to share in God's love (van Buren 1980, 8 and van Buren 1983, 59-60).

According to van Buren, God's decision to create had consequences not only for creation but for God as well. What Creation means for God is this: God is drawn into a relationship with creation in which God like creation itself is susceptible to time, and is basically to be viewed within a historical framework. In other words, God along with everything in creation has a past, a present, and a future that is to be described in terms of a relationship between the Creator and creation. We might put it this way: God's past is God's act of Creation. God's present is God's interaction with creation. God's future can be understood in two senses: (1) Because God is an entity in history, which, as we shall see, also means an entity in space and time— God has a body — God's future can mean simply what God does and what happens to God tomorrow and the next day, etc. (2) But God's future might also be taken in an ultimate sense as the goal towards which history moves, or, at least towards which God intends for it to move.[2] Here God's (ultimate) future is coterminous with the redemption of the world, the end of history.[3]

If God's decision to create heaven and earth was an act that at least in some important ways determined God, determined God in relation to creation and God's involvement in creation, God's act of Creation was, obviously, determining of creation, too. For van Buren, it was the purpose and intent of God that creation be "in the beginning" incomplete or unfinished. The more traditional Christian teaching about Creation is that God created a world that was a perfect primodial paradise. That the world we all know does not fit that idealic notion is attributed not to God, but to human sin, "the Fall." In much Christian teaching life is understood as an attempt to return to or regain that which was lost. For van Buren, what we seek is not something we have lost, but something we have yet to realize. God created the world unfinished. Its completion, its perfection, lies out ahead of us. It may be in our future; in any event, it is not a part of our past (van Buren 1983, 89-90).

1.1 God and Other Persons.

Humanity also was a part of God's original act of Creation. Van Buren interprets, "Then God said, "Let us make man in our image, after our likeness" (Gen. 1:26a), to mean that God created human beings persons as God is a person(van Buren 1983, 95-7).

Van Buren uses the Barthian notion of God as normative person. By God as normative person van Buren means, "God is that one unique Person by whom we measure what it is for us to be persons" (van Buren 1980, 102-104). In other words, to say that God is a person is not to use the language of analogy. It is not that God is like us a person, but rather, we are made persons in the likeness of the God who is the normative person.

We have said that van Buren for theological reasons wishes to present the Creation story, and indeed the whole of the story that the Hebrew Bible tells, not in a way a Christian might tell the story (a Christian interpretation), but rather as a Jew might tell the story (a Jewish interpretation). To this end one of the things van Buren wishes to do is to affirm what he takes to be the Jewish notion of a person as a mind-bodied unity. Nevertheless, he does not limit himself to Jewish sources for this view. For example, he uses the Strawsonian notion that the concept of a person is basic (van Buren 1980, 105)[4], to support the view of a person as a mind-body unity. If the concept of a person is basic, then it is logically prior to the concept of a self or a soul. Also, that a person has a body is part of the meaning of what it is to be a person, i.e. it is analytic to the concept of a person that a person has a body. This undercuts the notion of mind (self, soul) body dualism of Plato and Descartes, as it undercuts the classical Christian teaching that a person is essentially a soul.

An implication of using Strawson's concept of a person is that God too must be viewed as having a body. Van Buren does not shy away from this implication; indeed, he seems quite easily to embrace it. He claims that there are only three alternatives to the question whether God has a body: (1) God does not have a body, that is, God is disembodied, which is the classical tradition of both Christianity and Judaism, (2) God has the world for God's body, and (3) God is embodied in a way that is hidden. Van Buren dismisses (1) as being inconsistent with the Strawsonian concept of a person. He dismisses (2) as being inconsistent with God as the Creator of the world in which God and the world, i.e. persons in the world, are personally related. If God is related to the world in the way that selves are related to their bodies, this is not a personal relationship, so God's relationship to the world is not personal. Van Buren opts for (3). (3) also like (1) and (2) is incoherent. But (3)'s incoherence lies with the concept of God's embodiment — God's body is normally unseen, does not prevent God from being present in more than one place at a time, and seems to be unrestricted as to motion and location — not in the personal conception of God. Van Buren opts for (3) because the other two make reference to God as a person incoherent, while (3) does not; and van Buren is committed, metaphysically committed, to viewing reality as basically that of interpersonal relationship between God, the Creator and normative person, and a world of persons, God's creation (van Buren 1980, 108-111).

1.2 Sin.

Also part of the Creation story is the story of Adam and Eve, which in the classical Christian tradition introduces "the Fall" and "original sin." Because of the sin of Adam and Eve, all of humanity is under the condition of Sin; we are born into Sin. We are "lost" and by our very nature "fallen." Being cut off from God we cannot by our own effort return to God. But along with the problem that the church formulates comes also the answer to it: It was only by God's own act in Jesus Christ that a way was created for us to return to God, that way being God's gift of faith in Jesus Christ. But, of course, this teaching will not do for a Christian theology that wishes to acknowledge the eternal covenant between God and Israel. If Israel is in covenantal relationship with God that began before the coming of Christ and continues to this day — the covenant is eternal — then the meaning of Christ cannot be the solution to a problem that began in the Garden of Eden; or, at the very least, it cannot be the only solution.

Van Buren repudiates the Augustinian notion of "Original Sin." As persons human beings are made by God able to respond to God and responsible to God. The ability of persons to respond to God was not lost with Adam's sin, according to van Buren. Adam's sin was simply the first sin. Others have followed, and others will follow. But the first sin, Adam's sin, is not the cause of those that have and will follow (van Buren 1983, 96, 104).

Van Buren defines sin as the refusal of the choice that God has chosen for God's creatures (van Buren 1983, 104). We have an evil inclination to make the wrong choices, according to van Buren, and this is a real threat to creation; indeed sin introduces an element of chaos that threatens creation right at its center (van Buren 1983, 103). But we can overcome our evil inclination by responding to God. We have not yet introduced van Buren's important notion of covenant. Still, we need to introduce at least an element of it here, namely that of God calling us, which in turn calls for a response from us. What van Buren is claiming is that Adam's sin didn't preclude us from hearing and responding to God, and that within the relationship established in the hearing and responding (the covenant) our evil inclination can be overcome (van Buren 1983, 104-5).

1.3 Unfinished Creation.

We have said that according to van Buren God created the world unfinished, incomplete. God did this because God wishes our help, our cooperation, our partnership with God, in completing what God has on God's own but started; Creation is a start, a beginning. Indeed, according to van Buren, God determined from the beginning that creation would not be finished, would not come to completion without our (all of humanity's) cooperation. God made us with the ability to respond to God and responsible to God, so that we might with God complete the creation of the world. We are along with God responsible for whether the world reaches its completion. We are also responsible along with God for the path the world takes at any given time. History according to van Buren is the interaction, the mutual interaction of God and the World, the Creator and creation, God and God's creatures.

The question can now be put, will the world reach completion, will creation be finished, will the world be redeemed? For van Buren, the answer to this question is, there is no guarantee that it will. God wills the world's completion, which for van Buren means the same thing as the world's redemption. But God has decided that it will not be determined by God alone, not something God will do on God's own, but rather only with our cooperation. There is real risk in the enterprise that God has begun but has decided will not be finished without our help. The completion of the world is not inevitable; failure is possible; redemption is not assured (van Buren 1983, 99-100). [5]

1.4 An After-Life.

Traditional Christian teaching understands persons, as we have already said, as essentially souls, indeed immortal souls which at death leave their bodies and go on to their eternal destinies, go on to spent eternity in Heaven or Hell. Van Buren understands the doctrine of Creation to be less a story of origins and more a narrative confession of reality (Van Buren 1983, 44). Heaven and Hell do not exist in the reality that van Buren finds in the Creation story. What exists is God and God's creation. Heaven and Hell are not a part of creation, not a part of the world, and other than God, the world is the only reality there is. To this extent we may say that van Buren's theology of the Jewish-Christian reality views Judaism and Christianity as this-worldly religions.

Does this mean that there is no after-life in van Buren's scheme of things? Van Buren's says very little about an after-life, but his thought seems to be this: Death is sleep. Does one ever awaken from this sleep? The answer to this is, maybe. There is the general resurrection of the dead in "the World to Come," but what this rabbinic notion means for van Buren is the world as it will come to be, that is, this world, not some other world, not some reality different from the reality of this world. For van Buren, the expression "the World to Come" refers to the future in which this world finds completion, redemption. So, for van Buren with world redemption there is also the general resurrection of the dead. But there is no guarantee that there will be world redemption, and so no guarantee of an after-life either. Both depend on us in partnership with our Creator (van Buren 1983, 93 and 109).[6]

1.5 Summary.

Let us summarize van Buren's worldview, the structure of reality that he finds in the Creation story. Van Buren at least claims that this worldview is Israel's by its own testimony, and the Christian has but to hear it and confirm it.

The God we know is God our Creator. God intended that what God created would be but a beginning. This is so because it was part of God's purpose from the very beginning that what God started would only be completed with the cooperation of God's (human) creatures.

God is a person, or rather, the one normative person. God created human creatures persons as God God's self is a person; God and other persons have personal agency. Persons by definition have bodies and exist in space and time; God is no exception to this basic definition of what it is to be a person. The nature of God must be understood as self-determined in God's initial act of Creation.

God created us with the ability to sin. Sin is not choosing the choice that God intended for us. We don't sin because Adam sinned; Adam's sin was simply the first sin. Sin can be overcome by a (covenantal) relationship with God.

Sin is a threat to creation. More specifically sin is a threat to the goal of creation. God intends that what God started will be completed, that is to say, God will not give up on it. But it will only happen if we cooperate with God. We were created responsible for the world's redemption. It is because of this that there is no guarantee that the world will be redeemed. God is faithful to the goal of world redemption, but are we? World redemption is not inevitable, the whole enterprise can end in failure. Whether death is the end of our lives depends on the ultimate end. If the ultimate end is world redemption, then death is but sleep from which we rise at the End. If the ultimate end is failure, then death is sleep from which we never wake up; death is ultimate. Obviously no one including God knows what the actual End will be.

Reality is a personal God in interaction with God's creation. This interaction determines the path of what van Buren calls history. History is linear and finite — it moves in one direction and like a story has a beginning, a middle, and an end.[7] History has a purpose, a goal. All the actions of God, if not all our actions, are intended to move history towards its goal of world redemption.

There is one element in van Buren's scheme of things we have yet to introduce, namely the vehicle by which God and God's creation work together for the world's redemption, the covenant. It was for the sake of the covenant that God created in the first place. It is to a consideration of it that we turn next.

Chapter Six

A Theology of the Jewish-Christian Reality: The Covenant and Israel

God created the world unfinished because God determined in the beginning that what God had begun would only be completed, if it would be completed, not by God alone, but by God and God's creatures acting as co-workers in the task. World redemption would come about by the cooperative effort of God and the people of God. The vehicle for this cooperative effort is the covenant. Because God intended that creation only reach completion by our cooperating with God in the covenant, it can be said that Creation was for the sake of the covenant; God had the covenant in mind in God's act of Creation. The covenant is for the sake of redemption; redemption for the world, as well as for God. The covenant begins with Abraham, but because van Buren has his own unique and interesting interpretation of the purpose of the Noachide covenant, perhaps we should start with it.

1. The Noachide Covenant.

As we saw in Chapter Two, Judaism, particularly European Judaism of the Middle Ages, gave some validity and recognition to Christianity in terms of the Noachide covenant.[1] But van Buren believes that the Noachide covenant provides no adequate theological grounds for a Jewish understanding of the church. He views the Noachide covenant as not providing the means for the church to express its own experience of its personal relationship to God (van Buren 1983, 132). Its purpose then must be elsewhere.

For van Buren, Genesis 1 through 11 (and therefore also the story of Noah and the Noah covenant) tells a story of God and unfinished creation. In these chapters there is no indication as to how God is going to go about completing what God has begun; rather that occurs in Chapter 12 (the story of Abraham). Chapters 1-11 represent prehistory for van Buren, while with the call of Abraham history is introduced into creation. Chapters 1-11 set the stage for and point to Chapter 12.

According to van Buren it has taken God from the time of Adam to the time of Noah to realize what God's decision to create has meant for God, as well as for creation. What it has meant is that God is bound to God's creatures, and God's creatures are bound to God; God is our Creator, and we are God's (van Buren 1983, 134).

In the story of the Flood God has renewed creation. By doing this God shows, perhaps to God's self as well as to God's creation, that God will carry through what God had begun "in the beginning." God will not give up on creation; God will be bound to it as it is bound to God. Nevertheless, the flood did not really solve anything — a renewed creation is still unfinished and in need of completion. The renewed creation points ahead to its completion. This is its purpose; this is the purpose of the Noah story (van Buren 1983, 135).

According to van Buren, the covenant with creation made through Noah contains God's promise to the world of a future. But it also contains an invitation: "All of Noah's descendants, every nation or people is invited to see itself in the light of the special story of the one people that begins with the call of Abram" (van Buren 1983, 136). In other words, for van Buren it is at least possible that everyone can understand themselves not in terms of the Noachide covenant, but in terms of the one covenant that really matters, the covenant that begins with Abraham. How this is so, or how van Buren at least understands this to be so, especially since the story of the covenant is essentially a story that Israel tells about itself, we will have to consider in due course.

To summarize: Creation is made for the purpose of the one covenant, the one that really matters, the one that begins with Abraham. Creation is an act of God that did not result in a creation that was perfect and complete, but rather one that was but started. God intended from the beginning that creation itself would participate in bringing about its own completion, its own redemption, by working with God in the context of the covenant. God intended the covenant from the beginning, and so creation itself was made for the covenant. But the covenant itself is not redemption, (although, as we shall see, participation in the covenant, whether it be through the door and gift of Torah, or the door and gift of Jesus Christ, is proto-redemptive). The purpose of the covenant is to provide the vehicle by which God and God's creatures together might bring creation to completion. The purpose of the covenant is world redemption.

The Noah story and the Noah covenant is part of the Creation story. It is part of the story of God and unfinished creation (Genesis 1-11), a story which sets the stage and points toward redemption's vehicle (Genesis 12), the one covenant. But the Noah story and covenant is not itself a part of redemption's story. For this reason, the Noachide covenant is not adequate for understanding Christianity. Therefore its purpose must be other than that. For van Buren its purpose is to help set the stage for the only genuine covenant, the one that begins with Abraham.

2. The Abrahamic Covenant.

For van Buren the story of Abraham is Israel's story (van Buren 1983, 117-118). It is also the story of the church. How and in what sense the story of Abraham is the church's story will be addressed in the next chapter, Chapter Seven. Our present concern is with van Buren's understanding of the covenantal determination of the people, Israel.

According to van Buren Israel understands itself, understands its story, as beginning with the story of Abraham. But, for van Buren, to say this is also to say: (1) that the covenant begins with Abraham, and (2) that history begins with Abraham. What we want to do is to understand how and in what sense Israel, the covenant, and history all begin with Abraham's story.

For van Buren, Israel is primarily to be defined by its election:

> God's election of Israel is the foundation for everything that Israel has
> to say, and for its continuing existence as his witness. Everything else
> in Israel's life and testimony follows from this; nothing precedes or
> leads up to it. Israel is the people of God or it is nothing(van Buren
> 1983, 116).

> Faithful and unfaithful, willing and unwilling, this people is defined by
> God's election" (van Buren 1983, 123).

> One either stands upon Israel's own theological tradition and takes this
> people to be the people of God by God's election..., or one does not"
> (van Buren 1983, 162).

Israel, according to van Buren, understands its own story to have
begun with Abraham in the sense that the Abraham story is the story of
election, Israel's election (van Buren 1983, 118). Indeed, it is with the
use of the notion of election that van Buren ties together Israel, the
covenant, and history as all getting started with Abraham.

Election means recruitment, recruitment for a task(van Buren 1983,
118). In other words, election has a purpose, and according to van
Buren, the story of Abraham is the story of God's purpose for his
unfinished creation (van Buren 1983, 118). But this is also the purpose
of the covenant. For van Buren the covenant gets started with the
Abraham story because this is where election begins, or said another
way: what constitutes the covenant beginning with Abraham is the
same thing that constitutes Israel's story beginning with Abraham,
namely election.

For van Buren history also begins with election (van Buren 1983,
137). We have already stated that what van Buren means by history is
an interaction between the Creator and the Creator's creatures. But
perhaps now it is clearer that what van Buren means by history is what
we might call salvation history (Heilsgeschichte). For van Buren,
Abraham as the elect one, initiates the actual path of redemption.
History is understood as a path created by the interaction of the electing
God and God's elect (van Buren 1983, 116). History is not just the
interaction of God and God's creatures, it is the interaction of God and
God's people, it is interaction in the covenant, it is interaction for the
purpose of redemption. History, just as Israel and the covenant, gets
started with the story of Abraham, when that story is understood as the
story of election.

3. The Covenant of Sinai: Torah and its Role.

For van Buren, there is one covenant, a covenant that got started with Abraham. But what then of the covenant of Sinai and the giving of Torah? According to Scripture (the Exodus story), God became Israel's God and Israel became the people of God at Sinai. Also, van Buren must contend with the rabbinic tradition which seems to understand Israel's election to be based on its acceptance of Torah:

> If it were not for my Torah which you accepted, I should not recognize you, and I should not regard you more than any of the idolatrous nations of the world." (Exodus P., Ki Tissa, 47:3) (Montefiore and Loewe, 1974, 116).

Why is Israel called God's people? Because of the Torah." Rabbi Jose ben Shimon says: "Ere you stood at Sinai and accepted my Torah, you were called Israel, just as other nations...are called by simple names, without addition. But when you accepted the Torah at Sinai, you were called "My People," as it says, "Hearken, O my People, and I will speak" (Psalms 50:7) (Tan. B., Wa'ha, 9a) (Montefiore and Loewe 1974, 81).

> It says in Lev. 11:45, "For I am the Lord Your God who brought you up out of the land of Egypt to be your God: ye shall therefore be holy, for I am holy." That means, "I brought you out of Egypt on the condition that you should receive the yoke of the commandments." (Sifra 57a) (Montefiore and Loewe 1974, 117).

Van Buren attempts to maintain Israel's election as an inheritance from Abraham, while at the same time giving a central position to Sinai, by seeing Torah not as a condition of election, but rather as its "concrete form."

> Life in the Torah is the concrete form of its election. Election, for Israel, is an incarnate reality. It happens in the flesh, in Israel's flesh, and so it takes the form of walking, of halakhah, according to God's Torah (van Buren 1983, 157).

Elsewhere van Buren talks about the election becoming "effective" at Sinai, (van Buren 1983, 159) and Torah as the "shape" that election takes (van Buren 1983, 157). Further, van Buren is not unaware that other covenants appear in the Scriptural story; for example, the covenant of Shechem (Josh. 24:1-27) and the covenant of David (2 Sam. 23:5). But, for him, these other covenants are but further expressions of Israel's Sinaitic relationship to its God (van Buren 1983, 155). And, again, the covenant of Sinai is but the covenant that began with Abraham given shape and becoming effective with the giving of Torah.

Van Buren does not view the Abraham story as involving revelation. This seems to be because for him revelation creates community (van Buren 1983, 159 and 217), and it is at Sinai that Israel becomes Israel, the people become the people. The Torah is God's revelation from Sinai that creates a community, the people Israel, and that sets the people on God's way into history (van Buren 1983, 159).

For van Buren what Torah refers to is both the Written Torah and the Oral Torah, the Hebrew Bible and the Talmud (van Buren 1983, 212). But he views the Torah as going even beyond this:

> Israel, the Jewish people, has lived by Torah and Torah has kept Israel together and alive. The Torah that has been so central to Jewish existence over the centuries, however, is not simply the Five Books of Moses, but the evolving, growing rabbinic interpretation of Torah, namely, the Talmud and the ongoing halakhic creativity of generation after generation of rabbis. This is what Israel means primarily by Torah (van Buren, 1983, 214).

The Torah is a gift from God, just as the covenant and election are gifts of God (van Buren 1983, 76 and 210). Torah observance is not a means of entering into the covenant, entering into the way of redemption. Rather, Torah observance sustains the people in the covenant; it is the means by which the people live in the covenant; it is the means by which the people walk with God (van Buren 1983, 76). This means that Torah supplies the support needed to overcome the evil inclination (van Buren 1983, 216).

If the history of Israel contains occurrences of the failure to live by Torah, occurrences in which the evil inclination held sway; still, God does not leave Israel without a remedy in such instances, but rather God makes an offer of teshuvah, repentance, turning back to God (van

Buren 1983, 160). Up to the time of the destruction of the Second Temple (70 C.E.) cultic sacrifices were what make repentance effective. But since the destruction and down to the present, it is the synagogue which has in effect replaced the Temple, and repentance and deeds of loving kindness have taken over the role of cultic sacrifices (van Buren 1983, 191). While van Buren is aware that there is a special time of repentance in the Jewish year, the High Holy Days, with their climax in the Day of Atonement, Yom Kippur; still, he understands the whole of Jewish life as that of repentance, a continuing turning back to God:

4. The Land, the State of Israel, and Zionism.

Because van Buren's position on the issues of the Land, the State of Israel, and Zionism are so diametrically opposed to the views of Rosemary Ruether, another important Christian participant to the Jewish-Christian dialogue (See Chapter Two), perhaps it would be worthwhile and a help in evaluating van Buren's views on these issues to compare and contrast van Buren's position with that of Ruether.

Fundamental to the different positions that van Buren and Ruether take is their understanding of the nature of Judaism itself. For Ruether, Judaism is a religion.[2] For van Buren, Judaism refers not to a religion but to a nation (van Buren 1983, 31, 159, 165, and 186).

For Ruether the claim that Judaism is a nation is a claim made by Zionists. Zionism is a movement that developed in the late 19th and early 20th century, which Ruether claims was shaped by European racial nationalism and colonialism of the time. For Ruether, Zionism is equated with racism; "nation" is understood in the sense of "race."[3]

For van Buren, Zionism is grounded in a long tradition of Diaspora longing for the restoration of the Jewish people in eretz Yisrael (van Buren 1983, 191). Zionism was not shaped by the pseudoscientific, late-nineteenth-century Germanic myth of "race"; Zionism does not understand "nation" in the sense of "race," as Ruether claims; Zionism is not racism. Rather, Zionism is a Jewish version of peoplehood-plus-place (van Buren 1983, 175-176).

For Ruether, the Diaspora is the normal state of the Jewish people. One thing she means by this is simply the historical fact that the Jewish people have existed outside the land of Israel more than they have existed on the land (Ruether 1989, 230). She seems to side with that part of the Jewish tradition that understands Diaspora as for the purpose of mission; so that the Diaspora is a normal state in this sense as well (Ruether 1989, 20 and 230). While van Buren acknowledges the historical fact that the Jewish people have existed in the Diaspora for a much longer period of time than on the land, he seems to side with the Jewish tradition that views the Diaspora as exile (Galuth). From this perspective, the Diaspora is not normal regardless of how long it has lasted (van Buren 1983, 169).

God had promised Abraham that he would become a great nation (Genesis 12:2) and that to his descendents God would give the land as an "everlasting possession" (Genesis 17:8). God made good on the first promise at Sinai; it was there that the people, Israel, was born. It is the case that for most of Israel's history it has not been in possession of the land. Nevertheless, it is van Buren's position that the former land of Canaan became by divine election the land of Israel, eretz Yisrael; and this is true whether Israel is in possession of it or not. The land is an integral part of God's covenant with Israel, and the present State of Israel is caught up in Israel's election and purpose (van Buren 1983, 184, 187, and 202). But, does this mean as Ruether claims it means that "no other people, whether they may have dwelt there for centuries or millennia, have any right to this land?" (Ruether 1989, 214). First, we should note that van Buren nowhere explicitly states this. The question is, is this implied by what he does say? We think the answer to this question should be, no. We can give at least two reasons for our answer: (1) van Buren claims that all revelation is shrouded in ambiguity. The content of revelation has an element of uncertainty about it, and because of this, the recipients of revelation are reminded that they are called in their creaturely freedom to decide God's will and purpose in specific situations (van Buren 1983, 188). (2) Ruether claims that van Buren views Israel as called to a higher destiny than other nations, called to be an exemplar to the nations (Ruether 1989, 214). Van Buren explicitly denies that he views Israel in this way. Israel has a role of witness to the other nations, but that role does not take the form of model (van Buren 1983, 198). We shall have more to say about van Buren's view on Israel's mission, but for the present let us just say that it includes reminding the nations that God gives a place to them, just as God gives a place to Israel (van Buren 1983, 195). In other words, van Buren does take the position that Israel has a theological claim to the land, but this does not mean for van Buren that Israel has an a priori superior claim to it. Within the context of van

Buren's understanding of Israel's mission, and again we will go into more detail as to what that mission is a little later, other nations could make similar claims. Israel's theological claim to the land is not decisive. Van Buren's point is not to say something about who has a better claim to the land, but rather to say something about Israel, namely, that land and the State of Israel have theological significance for Israel; God's covenant with Israel includes the Promised Land and the State of Israel; the definition of Israel is not complete without including in it the Land and the State of Israel.

Van Buren is aware of the injustices shown Arab Israelis by the government of Israel (van Buren 1983, 186), as well as of the injustice of Israel being an occupying power in the territories (van Buren 1983, 204).[4] Nevertheless, van Buren is particularly silent about the plight of the Palestinian people. In contrast, the whole work of Ruether in *The Wrath of Jonah* (1989) seems to have as its purpose precisely that; precisely the plight of the Palestinian people, particularly those under the military rule of the Israeli army, Palestinians of the occupied territories Still, it would be unfair to judge van Buren on this point when he is writing on this subject before the Intifada, before the Palestinian uprising that began in December of 1987, and that brought the plight of the Palestinians into focus.

Van Buren certainly favors the Israeli side of the Israeli-Palestinian conflict; just as Ruether clearly favors the Palestinian side. Van Buren hears the Israeli side better than the Palestinian side, while the reverse is true for Ruether. Let us give one example in which van Buren seems to hear only the Israeli side: Van Buren's characterization of the Arab-Israeli conflict of 1948 as a conflict in which Israel was up against "insuperable numerical and material odds" is certainly the Israeli perception of things at the time (van Buren 1980, 154 and 181). Nevertheless, such a characterization probably does not fit the facts.[5] Ruether is more right here than van Buren.[6] Still, Ruether, quite unfairly in our view, overstates the matter when she characterizes van Buren as nothing more than a propaganda arm of the government of the State of Israel (Ruether 1989, 214-15). Van Buren certainly believes that the church owes a service to the Jewish people with such service including service to the State of Israel. (On this point we will have more to say later, after we have presented van Buren's view of the covenant and Christianity.) Still, van Buren would flatly deny that such service excludes the church from taking a critical stand on the behavior of the Israeli government.[7]

Ruether's view on the Jewish people is that they are a global religious community, some of which are, simply as a matter of fact, Israelis by nationality (Ruether 1989, 230). For Ruether, there is no special problem relating the Diaspora to the State of Israel; it is certainly not a theological problem. But this is not so for van Buren. Van Buren's view is that the State of Israel is the place where the people are to live their covenant with God. But if this is so, what about the Diaspora, when now it has a state of its own, but chooses not to go to it, chooses not to make aliyah?

First, van Buren sees this issue---the issue of the proper relationship between the Diaspora and the State of Israel — as an issue that is in dispute within the Jewish community itself, and as such is not something that is the duty of a Christian theologian to settle (van Buren 1983, 196 and 201). Nevertheless, after making the observation that the Zionist goal of a total aliyah of all the Jewish people seems not to represent the present reality of the whole house of Israel's under-standing of how it is to live in its covenant with God, and after depicting the relationship as complex, van Buren finally characterizes the relationship this way: "...within the fundamental unity that overarches all differences, the Diaspora supports the Jewish state upon which its own Diaspora existence depends" (Ruether 1989, 318-19).

Let us conclude this section by making a judgment as to who has the better view, Ruether or van Buren. The heart of the disagreement between Ruether and van Buren we believe lies in the first place in their quite different understanding of Judaism itself. They also differ dramatically in their understanding of the Zionist movement, and what Zionism means. Ruether's view of Judaism as a religion is part of a Post-Enlightenment tradition that assumes the separation of religion from the political process. This may be appropriate in terms of viewing many religions, including Christianity. But is it appropriate for viewing Judaism? The claim that Judaism is a nation Ruether sees as a Zionist claim that was formed and developed within the context of 19th century European views of nationalism and colonialism. Van Buren would claim that Ruether is not listening to the Jewish witness to itself. Van Buren claims that throughout the history of Israel's witness it has viewed itself as a nation. The Enlightenment and Emancipation may have complicated the issue according to van Buren, but he at any rate sees no reason for changing the definition of Judaism because of those events. Zionism did not create the definition of Judaism as a nation, it simply recognized a long tradition of Israel's own understanding of itself. In our opinion van Buren has the better position: It is part of the definition of the Jewish people that they are a nation.

5. Israel's Mission.

Ruether argues that the myth of the Promised Land is used by Zionists to claim a superior right to the land. She further argues that the myth itself should be rejected because it presupposes a concept of God that is tribal and exclusive, and that already within the Bible that concept of God was being questioned in favor of a more Universalist concept of God as creator of nations (Ruether 1989, 234).

It may be that some Zionists argue the way that Ruether claims. But, while it is the case that van Buren argues for Israel's right to the land on theological grounds, we have argued that this does not mean, for van Buren, that such an argument is decisive. We have argued this for two reasons, (1) revelation for van Buren is always ambiguous and in need of human interpretation based on the circumstances of the present, and (2) because of the message contained in Israel's mission. We now wish to elaborate on van Buren's understanding of Israel's mission.

Israel believes itself to have been taken into a covenant with God by which it became co-workers with God for the purpose of completing what God with Creation had but begun. For van Buren, Israel furthers the purpose of the covenant, furthers the completion of the world, in two ways: First, Israel serves the purpose of the covenant by living in the covenant; and, as we have seen, Israel lives in the covenant by living according to God's Torah. Israel serves the purpose of the covenant by being itself, by being what God has called it to be. This serves the purpose of the covenant by presenting the world with a sign of the reality of the one God. The mission of Israel to the world is to be a witness to God, and it performs this mission by being itself, by being faithful to its calling (van Buren 1983, 206-7).

The purpose of Israel's bearing witness to the world to the reality of God is not that the world might become a part of Israel, however. Israel's mission is not to convert the nations to Judaism, according to van Buren, although he does not mean by this that Israel would prevent anyone who would want to from joining the Jewish people (van Buren 1983, 178).

Israel's mission to the nations is not only bearing witness to the reality of God. Israel also has a message for the nations. The message is this: Just as God has called the Jewish people in their particularity to cooperate with God in completing creation, so also does God wish to call the nations in their particularity into a cooperative effort as well. Further, just as the land is part of God's call to Israel, Israel's message to the nations is that God also provides for them a place, a land in which they are to live and cooperate with God for the furtherance of world redemption (van Buren 1983, 176, 195, and 198-9).

The question immediately arises, of course, what about when the same land is in dispute, as in the Israeli-Palestinian situation? Van Buren does not suggest a solution to the conflict. Still, we have argued that it is unfair to view van Buren's position as giving a superior theological claim to Israel. Such claims are ambiguous and always in need of interpretation in terms of immediate circumstances, on the one hand, and van Buren's position makes it possible for both sides to make similar theological claims, on the other. Ruether sees the possibility of a solution to the Israeli-Palestinian conflict only when both sides recognize the fact that they represent two national identities that have grown up in the same region (Ruether 1989, 130). The government of the State of Israel in the 1990s (during the period of the Rabin government) seems to be moving towards recognizing the national aspirations and identities of the Palestinians on the West Bank, something it had refused to do in the 1980s (during the period of the Shamir government). In van Buren's argument against the claim that the State of Israel has the obligation to provide for the Palestinians a land and a sovereign state, one could interpret van Buren to be saying that it is not Israel's obligation alone, but Israel's together with the Arab states in the region. This implies that van Buren gives recognition to Palestinian national identity. He seems to take the position that only when the Arab states follow Egypt's lead and recognize and accept the existence of the State of Israel, can the Palestinian question then be addressed. At the time in which he was writing (the early 1980s), he seemed not to see as a possibility direct negotiations between the Israelis and the Palestinians (van Buren 1983, 303).

6. Summary.

Van Buren views Israel as defined by its covenantal relationship with God. A relationship that got started with Abraham and has continued ever since — the covenant is eternal. But, not only Israel's story and the story of the covenant get started with the story of Abraham, history gets started with Abraham, as well.

History gets started with the Abraham story because what van Buren means by history is what might be called salvation history. History is God and Israel working together for the purpose of completing the creation. God had certainly been involved with creation and God's creatures before the Abraham story, but nowhere in that involvement was there any indication how God was going to involve others in the task of completing the unfinished world. This only gets stared with Abraham, and so, for van Buren, this is where history begins. History is the interaction of God and the Jewish people for the purpose of redeeming the world, which, for van Buren, means the same thing as for the purpose of the world's completion. It is difficult to distinguish between the covenant and history. We might view it this way: history is the path that the covenant takes.

God's approach to others is a covenantal approach. We are certainly not finished with considering what this important notion of covenant means for van Buren. But so far we have seen that van Buren views it as a relationship between God and the creatures of God. The relationship is initiated by God for the purpose of involving others in completing creation; God has decided that creation will be completed, if it ever will be completed, through the cooperation of others in a covenantal relationship with God.

The covenant gets started with Abraham because it is in the story of Abraham that van Buren sees for the first time God acting for the purpose of finishing what God had begun by God's act of Creation. But the purpose of finishing what God began is the purpose of the covenant, the one covenant; and so, the covenant gets started with Abraham.

The story of Abraham is also the beginning of Israel's story. Van Buren views the Abraham story as a story of Israel's election. Indeed, it is viewing the story as a story of election that allows van Buren to tie together history, covenant, and Israel's story as all getting started with the Abraham story.

Van Buren views Israel as being defined by its covenantal relationship with God. But in the context of covenant the two most important elements are election and Torah. Israel traces its election to the Abraham story; Israel's story gets started with its election. But Israel's life of election is "formed," made "concrete," "shaped," and made "effective" on the basis of Torah. This is the way in which van Buren views the Abraham story and the Exodus-Sinai story as one story, the Abrahamic covenant and the Sinai covenant as one covenant.

As the covenant and election are gifts of God received, so is Torah a revelatory gift of God to Israel. Torah is not a means into the covenant, rather it is the means by which the Jewish people are sustained in the covenant.

The extent of Torah is not just the first five books of the Hebrew Bible, nor the Hebrew Bible itself, nor even the Hebrew Bible and the Talmud, but rather includes as well, "...the ongoing halakhic creativity of generation after generation of rabbis."

The Torah supplies the support the Jewish people need to overcome the evil inclination. This does not mean though that sin is absent from the lives of the Jewish people. A decisive mark of Jewish life is repentance and God's continuous offer of repentance.

For van Buren, the land of Israel and the present State of Israel are caught up in the election and purpose of Israel. The covenant includes the land; the present State of Israel is a part of the people, Israel. For van Buren, the Jewish people are a nation. His argument for this view is that throughout Israel's long history this has been its predominant witness to itself.

Although van Buren recognizes that the Diaspora since the founding of the State of Israel is a Diaspora-by-choice, still he gives more weight to the Jewish tradition that views the Diaspora as galuth than to the Jewish tradition that understands the Diaspora as for the purpose of mission. Zionism for van Buren is grounded in a long tradition of Diaspora longing for the restoration of the Jewish people in eretz Yisrael.

We have argued that although van Buren views the land of Israel and the present State of Israel theologically, this does not mean he believes that others have an inferior claim to the land. Van Buren does not suggest a solution to the Israeli-Palestinian conflict, and he is particularly silent on the plight of the Palestinians. But this may be due less to his bias in favor of the State of Israel, although we believe he does have such a bias, and more to the time in which he is writing (the early 1980s).

It is not possible to understand Israel's mission entirely without understanding the church's mission on the one hand, and the relationship of Judaism and Christianity to other religions, on the other. And, of course, we are not prepared as yet to consider either one of these. Nevertheless, something could be said of Israel's mission at this point.

Israel's mission is to witness to the reality of God. It performs this mission by being what it is called to be — a people living a Torah-shaped life. But beyond that Israel also has a message from God to the nations: God wishes to involve the nations in their particularity, as God has involved Israel in its particularity, for the sake of world redemption.

Chapter Seven

A Theology of the Jewish-Christian Reality: The Covenant and Christianity

The purpose of this chapter is to present van Buren's view about how Christianity gets incorporated into Israel's covenant. Van Buren views Jesus as a Jew whose ministry was to Israel. But he also views Jesus as the Lord of the church, the one who draws Gentiles into the covenant. Van Buren bridges the two — Jesus as having a ministry only to Israel, and Jesus as Lord of the Gentile church — and does so in a way that is not anti-Judaic, by giving a radically new interpretation to Paul. Van Buren opts for a basic continuity between the Jesus of history and the Christ of faith. The continuity is one of function: Just as Jesus in his earthly ministry brought people before God, Jesus Christ of the Gentile church does so now. Van Buren interprets Easter covenantally, and in a way that is consistent with his worldview. Easter is a beginning (the beginning of the church) and a hope (hope of world redemption).

1. Jesus.

In *The Secular Meaning of the Gospel,* van Buren depicted Jesus in general terms as the definitive free person. There is some continuity in van Buren's treatment of the historical Jesus from his secular period to his Jewish-Christian dialogue period; for example, in both periods van Buren views Jesus within an historical framework as a human being, as a person. The difference, or rather one of the differences, is that in the Jewish-Christian dialogue period van Buren narrows the contexts in which Jesus is to be defined. In defining the historical Jesus in *The Secular Meaning of the Gospel* van Buren does not even mention the fact that Jesus was a Jew; it seems not to be important. But in the Jewish-Christian dialogue period, this becomes very important. The first thing that van Buren wants to say about Jesus as a human being is that he was a Jew; and as a Jew that he lived within the context of the covenant between Israel and God. For van Buren of the Jewish-Christian dialogue period, it is only the Jewish Jesus, a Jesus understood within the context of the covenant, within the context of the story of Israel, that is a comprehensible Jesus. A Jesus defined in general terms, a Jesus as he was defined in *The Secular Meaning of the Gospel,* is an incomprehensible Jesus (van Buren 1988, 62).

But once one places Jesus within the context of Judaism, the immediate question seems to be: What was Jesus' attitude towards Judaism? Was Jesus antagonistic towards his own people, or not? For van Buren, the understanding of Jesus in an antagonistic relationship to his own people is the root of the church's anti-Judaic thinking and behavior. While this picture of Jesus is clearly the one given in all four canonical Gospels, van Buren nevertheless believes that this is a late development, and that there is an earlier witness recoverable from the New Testament which images Jesus in solidarity with his people. The antagonism itself actually developed between the early church and Judaism, with the antagonism then retrojected back into the story of Jesus which the church told:

> The result of the conflicts of some of the early communities (and the ones that were later to be classified as orthodox or catholic) with Judaism and Marcionism is that their versions of the things concerning Jesus of Nazareth were deeply influenced by their anti-Judaic and anti-Marcionite concerns. Their own rejection by the synagogue led them to interpret Jesus' violent end as the result of his having been rejected

by his people: the Jewish rejection of the followers of Jesus must have seemed to them to have been the inevitable consequence of a Jewish rejection of Jesus himself (van Buren 1988, 15-16).

Van Buren's position on Jesus and anti-Judaism is similar to the one we drew in Chapter Three. [3] For van Buren, the final editing of the New Testament depicts an anti-Judaic Jesus. But, again, there is also discoverable in the New Testament an early witness that depicts Jesus in solidarity with his people (van Buren 1983, 244-6, and van Buren 1988,60 and 63). Van Buren repudiates the anti-Judaic Jesus found in the New Testament, and affirms the Jesus in solidarity with his people, also found in the New Testament. He claims that this is what any post-Holocaust Christian theology must do (van Buren 1988, 16-17).

Van Buren views the historical Jesus as an eschatological prophet standing in the tradition of Jewish restoration theology. Jesus believed that the promises to Israel would soon be fulfilled: the eschatological restoration of Israel was at hand. Its completion in the near future would be brought about by a dramatic intervention by God (van Buren 1988, 42, 63, 86 and 131-2).[4] But this apocalyptic perspective does not fit well into van Buren's worldview,[5] and so he gives a functional analysis of its language:

> An honest response to the gap between the eschatology of the witness to Jesus (and presumably of Jesus himself) and the continuing history of the "old" era to this day is to admit that, in so far as this witness presented Jesus as a herald of God's future as *future,* it made the mistake of many of that time and culture, against which Jesus is presented also as having warned: trying to discern a divine timetable. But as a herald of that future as God's *present*, Jesus poses today just the issue that he posed then in proclaiming God's reign at hand. The language of the future is ineradicably a part of that proclamation and so we shall continue to use it, but its use, its function, was to focus on the present. The moral, social, political, and personal immediacy of God was and remains the matter at stake in the apostolic witness to the preaching of the coming reign of God (van Buren 1988, 133).

Jesus' perspective might have been apocalyptic, he might have had the conviction that the reign of God was about to begin. But, according to van Buren, the language in which this perspective is expressed functions to place the one who hears it before God; its purpose is to make God present. For van Buren, Jesus was a Jew committed to the renewal of his people in their covenant with God, and he effected this renewal, in those in which he did effect it, by presenting them with the immediacy of God (van Buren 1988, 43, 89, and 110 and van Buren 1983, 255, 264).

2. Jesus Christ.

> The message of Jesus is a presupposition for the theology of the New Testament rather than a part of that theology itself. For New Testament theology consists in the unfolding of those ideas by means of which Christian faith makes sure of its own object, basis, and consequences. But Christian faith did not exist until there was a Christian kerygma; i.e., a kerygma proclaiming Jesus Christ — specifically Jesus Christ the Crucified and Risen One — to be God's eschatological act of salvation. He was first so proclaimed in the kerygma of the earliest church, not in the message of the historical Jesus, even though that church frequently introduced into its account of Jesus' message, motifs of its own proclamation. Thus, theological thinking — the theology of the New Testament — begins with the kerygma of the earliest church and not before. But the fact that Jesus had appeared and the message which he had proclaimed were, of course, among its historical presuppositions; and for this reason Jesus' message cannot be omitted from the delineation of New Testament theology (Bultmann 1951 and 1955, 3).[6]

This is the famous passage from Bultmann's *Theology of the New Testament* in which is expressed the radical discontinuity between the Jesus of history and the Christ of faith. In another place Bultmann gives but the barest connection between the historical Jesus and the Risen Christ (Bultman 1964, 20). In *The Secular Meaning of the Gospel* van Buren accepted this Bultmannian view of discontinuity. For van Buren, the discontinuity was expressed this way: Jesus' freedom only became "contagious" with Easter. Before Easter it was only Jesus that was free; that is to say, the historical Jesus did not spread the freedom he possessed. It was the Risen Lord whose freedom was "contagious"; it was the Risen Lord who spread the freedom that Jesus had exhibited in his earthly life. There is a radical discontinuity in the authority of Jesus and Jesus Christ. Before Easter, only Jesus exhibits freedom; after Easter, the Risen Lord spread the freedom Jesus had; after Easter, Jesus' freedom becomes "contagious."[7]

In his Jewish-Christian dialogue period, van Buren, relying on the work of Willi Marxsen,[8] chooses to understand a basic continuity between the Jesus of history and the Christ of faith, between Jesus and the story about Jesus, i.e. the gospel message (van Buren 1988, 40-41):

> The proclamation by the early church of Jesus was of one who proclaimed that the reign of God was at hand. Those are his opening words as he is presented in what is broadly thought to be the first of our extant Gospels. (Mk 1:15)

> The coming of God's reign is the recurring theme of parables and sayings attributed to him by the whole Synoptic tradition, just as his acts of healing are signs of the new era already effective in his actions. The witness of this tradition is to a Jesus who announced and confronted people with the immediacy of God's healing presence. (van Buren 1988, 49)

In *The Secular Meaning of the Gospel* what defined Jesus was freedom, freedom which was discontinuous between Jesus and Jesus Christ. In the Jewish-Christian dialogue period, freedom is still an important concept for van Buren, both for defining Judaism and defining Christianity (van Buren 1983, 225), but freedom is no longer the concept for defining Jesus. Now, in the Jewish-Christian dialogue period, Jesus is viewed as a vehicle by which people are placed before God. But just as Jesus brought people before God in his earthly ministry, the story about Jesus, which is the ministry of the church, brings the believer before God. In other words, there is a functional continuity between Jesus and the story about him. Just as the historical Jesus confronted people with the immediacy of God, so in the church Jesus Christ confronts people with the immediacy of God: "To hear the story of Jesus and to find oneself confronted by God is to understand the story and know it as the power of God," (van Buren 1988 19, 23, 36, 41, 42, 45, 60, 80, 82, 87 93, 94, 96, and 100).

3. The Gentile Church: Jesus Christ as the door into the covenant for Gentiles as Gentiles.

Jesus was a human being; but more specific than that, Jesus was a Jew. He is to be understood within the context of the Judaism of his own time. His audience was his own people, and what he presented them with was the immediacy of God. For those who were the recipients of this immediacy of God through Jesus, whether before Easter in his person, or after Easter in the story about him, there was born a renewed faith in God, a renewed commitment to the covenant; Jesus led, or attempted to lead, a renewal movement within Israel. This is van Buren's view of Jesus (van Buren 1988, 43, 89, and 112 and van Buren 1983, 254-58).

Just as Jesus in his earthly life and in the early church confronted his people with the immediacy of God, so does Jesus Christ today, in the context of the church, confront the hearer with the gift and claim of God (van Buren 1988, 23). But now the audience has changed. The church today is predominantly a Gentile church; and, indeed, what perhaps began as a renewal movement within Israel, relatively quickly became Gentile Christianity. The question is not how this happened, which may itself be a very complicated historical question, but rather, given van Buren's view of Jesus, why this happened. Why should there be a Gentile church? Why should not all Jesus' later disciples follow him as did his first disciples, as members of Israel? Why should not every "Christian" become a Jew? The answer to this question certainly cannot come from an understanding of Jesus or his message; Jesus is to be understood within the context of Judaism, and his message was addressed to his own people. Van Buren's answer to this question is Paul.

As we have seen, van Buren was able to gain a foothold in the New Testament for his theology of the Jewish-Christian reality by claiming that there exists within the text a Jesus that was not anti-Judaic — such an anti-Judaic Jesus does exist in the text, but this is a Jesus of the final editing of the text, a Jesus imaged by the early church that was in active conflict with Judaism. There exists another Jesus, a Jesus in solidarity with his people; a Jesus that served Israel. Such a Jesus as this is based on a reconstruction of the text, particularly that of the Synoptic Gospels. Van Buren's use of Paul, however, is not based on a reconstruction of the relevant texts, but rather is based on a radically new interpretation of Paul. As we have mentioned before, traditionally Paul has been understood as anti-Judaic. Indeed, all three Christian participants to the Jewish-Christian dialogue, that we considered in Chapter Three in our attempt to give some sense to the dialogue on the Christian side, take the traditional view of Paul, and so do not find him helpful in making a contribution to the dialogue. But van Buren does view Paul as helpful. Indeed, for van Buren, Paul is most important.

Van Buren not only gains a foothold in the New Testament for his theology of the Jewish-Christian reality in his view of Jesus, but he also finds a foothold for his theology in Paul. Indeed, as we shall see, it is van Buren's reading of Paul that motivates him to present a one covenant theory as the heart of his theology of the Jewish-Christian reality. For van Buren, it is Paul and not Jesus that validates the Gentile church. The challenge, of course, is to view Paul as doing this without being anti-Judaic in the process.[9] Our task now is to present van Buren's understanding of Paul: how Gentiles as Gentiles through their faith in Jesus Christ are drawn into, are included in, the covenant.

Israel understands its story to have begun with Abraham. Though as a people its life began at Sinai, its election began with Abraham, and so also its story; so also does the covenant and (salvation) history begin with Abraham. In the Abraham story God makes three promises to Abraham and to his descendants: (1) the promise that Abraham will become a great nation (Gen. 12:2), (2) the promise of the land (for example, Genesis 12:6-7), and (3) the promise that Abraham would be the father of many nations (Genesis 17:5).

God fulfilled the first promise at Sinai. God fulfilled the second promise when Israel took possession of the land; this fulfillment, besides the events of biblical times, might also be understood to include the events that led to the present state of Israel — Israel taking possession of the land again after a long exile. The fulfillment of the third promise Israel might understand as occurring, if it ever does occur, when the nations come to a relationship with God through Israel's witness. But this is not the way Paul understands the fulfillment of this promise. For Paul, the third promise was made to Abraham while he was still a Gentile, while the other two promises were made to him as a Jew. For Paul, the fulfilling of the promise to the Gentile Abraham that he would be the father of many nations was taking place through the preaching of Paul to the Gentiles. Paul's preaching announced that God had laid claim upon Gentiles in Jesus Christ. The message of Paul then is not the announcement of the end of covenantal fidelity to God through the Torah for Jews (the traditional interpretation), but rather the inclusion of Gentiles into that same covenant through their faith in Jesus Christ. Gentile inclusion in the covenant was intended by God from the beginning — it is there in the promise to Abraham. The fulfillment of that promise was happening by the Gentile response to the gospel that Paul preached (van Buren, 1983, 146-48 and 232-34).

The traditional anti-Judaic interpretation of Romans 10:4 ("For Christ is the end of the law...") is that with the coming of Christ, the time of the law (Torah) is ended; Christ abrogates the law. Van Buren would interpret Romans 10:4 this way: Christ is the end (of the negative effects) of Torah (for Gentiles). Van Buren makes use of a rabbinic story about how God had offered the Torah to the nations before God had offered it to Israel (van Buren 1983, 126). Israel accepted the Torah, but the nations had rejected it. Consequently, the nations were under the curse of the law (Torah); Torah functioned for Gentiles not within the covenant, but outside of it. Because of the nations' rejection of God's offer of Torah, it had only a negative effect on them. Christ is the end of the curse. Because Jesus Christ brought Gentiles into a covenantal relationship with God apart from Torah, this meant the end of the negative effects of Torah for Gentiles (van Buren 1983,232-4).[10]

The traditional view is that Paul's treatment of Torah is aimed at Jews and Judaism — Paul in his authentic letters is evaluating Judaism per se. The fact that the concept of repentance, a concept which is very important to Judaism as we have seen, never appears in Paul, has been explained by the traditional view in one of two ways: either Paul did not understand the Judaism of his own day, or he chose to ignore this aspect of Judaism. But van Buren, following Gaston and others who are involved in this new interpretation of Paul, has another explanation. What Paul was about was not the assessment of Judaism for Jews, but rather the legitimating of the inclusion of Gentiles as full-fledged members of the people of God in these lasts times. The reason Paul never spoke of repentance is because repentance means turning back to the God of the covenant, but Paul was interested in Gentiles turning to God for the first time (van Buren 1983, 233).[11] As we have seen, van Buren understands the Jewish response to Jesus to have been a sense of renewal, a renewed commitment to their covenantal life with God. But this would not be the Gentile response to Jesus (the gospel, the story of Jesus, the content of Paul's preaching to Gentiles) because it could not be. The Gentiles were those who were without hope and without God in the world:

> Therefore remember that at one time you Gentiles in the flesh, called
> the uncircumcision by what is called circumcision, which is made in
> the flesh by hands — remember that you were at that time separated
> from Christ, alienated from the commonwealth of Israel, and strangers
> to the covenants of promise, having no hope and without God in the
> world. (Ephesians 2:11-12)

For Gentiles Paul's preaching did not bring a renewal of faith, it
brought the birth of faith, faith in the God of Israel. Gentiles came to a
knowledge of Israel's God, a knowledge of God of the covenant, on
new terms, not on the terms of Torah, but on the terms of Jesus Christ
(van Buren 1988, 113).

Van Buren's explanation of the story of the church, inspired by his
new interpretation of Paul, is very similar to his explanation of Israel's
story. Just as Israel's story begins with the Jewish Abraham story, in
the sense of its election having originated with Abraham, so also does
the church's story begin with the Gentile Abraham story in the same
sense — its election originated with Abraham. But Israel's life, the life
of the people as a people, only begins at Sinai. It is the revelation at
Sinai — the giving of Torah — that creates community, that creates the
people a people. Torah gives shape to the people's lives; Torah makes
Israel's election effective. Something very similar is true for the
church: The church, as a community of believers out of many nations,
though it may have been elected with the Abraham story, only gains
life with the revelation of Easter, or more specifically, with what van
Buren calls the Easter-Pentecost event. But it is not Torah that gives
shape to the Christian life, it is not Torah that makes Christian election
effective; rather, it is Jesus Christ. Just as the theme of election made
the Abraham story and the Exodus-Sinai story one story, the story of
the covenant, so now, the same theme of election makes the Abraham
story and the Easter-Pentecost story one story, the story of the same
covenant, the story of the one covenant (van Buren 1983, 239 and
252).

We will need to say more later about how van Buren views the
relationship between Christianity and Judaism. But if that relationship
is one in which Gentiles are included in the covenant with Israel, we
should at this point at least say something about how van Buren
understands this inclusion of Gentiles. He began by understanding the
inclusion of Gentiles (Christians) as adopted Jews (van Buren 1972,
130).[12] And, if Christians are adopted Jews, then they are also a part of

Israel; Christians and Jews together make up Israel (van Buren, 1976, 71). But then van Buren seemed to recognize that this way of looking at the issue fails to acknowledge that Jews and Christians belong to different religious communities; Gentiles are in no sense Jews, but Gentiles. Therefore, in his theology of the Jewish-Christian reality, van Buren views the relationship between Christians and Jews as one of alongsidedness: The proper place of the church is alongside Israel, playing a cooperative role with Israel for the sake of the covenant's purpose, for the sake of world redemption (van Buren 1983, 8, 9, 111, 145-6, and 151-2).

According to van Buren, God intended from the beginning this relationship of alongsidedness of Israel and the church. God intended from the beginning for the church and Israel to cooperate for the sake of world redemption. In other words, for van Buren, as for the other Christian participants to the Jewish-Christian dialogue that we have considered — Parkes, Eckardt, and Ruether — the church's anti-Judaic tradition was a church error; it was not intended by God. For van Buren the origin of the error is not with Jesus, and not with Paul — a foothold for his theology of the Jewish-Christian reality in the New Testament is secure. For van Buren the error developed when Gentile Christians began telling Jews, who believed in Jesus, that Torah was no more to be followed by them. For van Buren what split Christians and Jews was not the issue of christology, but the issue of Torah (van Buren 1983, 34 and 272-77).

4. Easter.

In *The Secular Meaning of the Gospel* the significance of Easter was that it was the event that caused the freedom which Jesus exhibited in his life to become contagious: after Easter others began to exhibit at least some of the freedom that Jesus had had. In his secular period, van Buren understood early Christian resurrection-language to be used to express hope that Jesus' freedom which had become contagious after Easter might some day prevail on earth. In a secular view of reality there can be no literal sense to the resurrection. So, what does it mean? It means that the early disciples hoped that the freedom Jesus had in his life, might some day be "caught" by everyone everywhere. It is our task now to present van Buren's understanding of Easter not in the context of secularism, but in the context of the Jewish-Christian dialogue, in the context of what van Buren calls the Jewish-Christian reality.

Consistent with his worldview, van Buren views Easter as a covenantal event. As such, Easter is first an act of God; God acts first to initiate the covenant. But constitutive of the event as well is the disciples' response to God's action. What van Buren is attempting to do is to understand Easter in the same way as he understands Sinai. Just as for Israel covenantal life with God is an offer (act) made by God that requires Israel's acceptance of the offer (accepting the gift of Torah), so also for Christians covenantal life is God's offer which requires their acceptance (accepting the gift of Jesus Christ). Both actions — the act of God (offer) and the act of Christians (accepting the offer) — constitute the Easter event (van Buren 1988, 111).

Let us use again the story of the king signing into law a decree that frees everyone in the realm. The question traditionally is, when are the citizens free, when the king signs the decree, or when citizens are told of the new law and begin to act in a free manner? The (Barthian) objective view is that salvation is an act of God: one becomes free, whether one knows it or not, when the king signs the decree. The (Bultmannian) subjective view is that salvation is an experience of one who has heard the good news: one is free when one hears and responds positively to the message. What van Buren has done in his Jewish-Christian dialogue period is to combine the objective and subjective views: Easter is not simply an act of God, but neither is it simply a subjective experience of Christian believers. Rather, Easter is both an act of God and an act of Christian believers; both acts together are constitutive of the Easter event.

We have already learned that for van Buren salvation (redemption) speaks to the world, not to the individual, and is fully future. The Exodus-Sinai event is protoredemptive for Jews, and the Easter-Pentecost event is protoredemptive for Christians, and both communities experience in their lives in the covenant a foretaste of redemption (van Buren 1983, 69). But redemption itself is world redemption, and, because this has not yet happened, redemption is not a present reality, but a future possibility. The purpose of the covenant is to bring the world to completion (redemption, salvation) through the cooperative efforts of God and God's covenantal partners. If this is so, then for van Buren in his Jewish-Christian dialogue period, the significance of Easter cannot be the accomplishment of salvation:

salvation is world salvation, and Easter, whatever it accomplished, did not accomplish that.

For van Buren of the Jewish-Christian reality, Easter is a beginning and a hope; it is not an accomplished fact. Because Easter faith draws Gentiles into the covenant, Easter is the beginning of life in the covenant for Gentiles. Because Gentiles are drawn into the covenant through their faith in Jesus Christ, they are drawn into the purpose (hope) of the covenant. What Christians hope for, they also have the responsibility of working for — cooperating with God and Israel for the sake of world redemption. Jews and Christians share the same hope, as they share the same responsibility for what they hope for (van Buren 1988, 13 and 120-2).[13]

In van Buren's secular period resurrection-language could not be understood to be expressing literal truth because it did not fit with his secular view of reality. So van Buren gave a less than literal interpretation of Christian resurrection-language for a secular Christianity. A literal view of resurrection-language does not fit van Buren's view of the Jewish-Christian reality either; it does not fit his Jewish-Christian worldview. There is in this worldview the notion of the general resurrection, but this occurs, if it does occur, with world redemption. What we want to do now is to present how van Buren in his Jewish-Christian dialogue period understands the Easter proclamation: He is Risen.

What is important for van Buren about Jesus is not his person but his function; van Buren gives a functional interpretation of Easter (van Buren 1988, 36, 45, and 120). What is important for the church is that Jesus Christ continue to do for those in the church what he did for those that encountered him in his earthly life — he presents them with God. Easter is the event by which that function of Jesus did not end but continued in the story of Jesus. For van Buren the term "resurrection" is a poor choice for trying to understand what the disciples meant by Easter (van Buren 1988, 44). What they meant was that Jesus lives or is alive. But what does this mean?

> As Jesus in his preaching and actions confronted his hearers with the gift and claim of God's unlimited love, so Jesus proclaimed by his disciples confronted the hearers of his witnesses with the same gift and claim. Jesus made men and women into servants of God, after as well as before his death. He was alive. (van Buren 1988, 45)

Traditionally the church's hope has been the "sure and certain" hope of the resurrection. The resurrection of Jesus Christ means that death itself has been overcome. Death still reigns, but because Jesus overcame death, with his return we too will be resurrected from the sleep of death. We need but wait for this, because as Jesus' death was for us, so is his return for us. Jesus' return is the redemption of the world. It is not something that we do or can bring about. Our "sure and certain" hope then is based only on Jesus, and what he will do for us; and what he will do for us is based on what he has already done for us — his victory over death.

For van Buren, the ultimate hope of the church is not "sure and certain." Nor is the hope of the church based on Jesus (Jesus' return) acting unilaterally on our behalf. Neither of these things is consistent with van Buren's worldview. The hope of the church must be world redemption. But there is no guarantee that that will occur — it is not sure and certain. If it does occur, it will not be because Jesus did something on his own, but because God and God's covenantal partners cooperated to bring the world to completion, to redemption. For van Buren, Easter is not a victory for God nor for the church. What Easter does mean is that God is persistent in God's covenantal purpose. Easter means that the cause of God, which is the only cause that Jesus had, will continue. It will continue in a new way, although the new way was promised by God beforehand in the Abraham story (van Buren 1988, 120-1). It will continue with Gentile inclusion. It will continue with the church alongside Israel creating with God the story of the covenant, the purpose of which is world redemption. God's cause will continue. But the story, now with new partners, is not finished; world redemption is not a reality (van Buren 1988, 123-5). Nothing is completed with Easter. Easter is a beginning (the beginning of the church) and a hope (hope of world redemption).

5. Summary.

For van Buren in his Jewish-Christian dialogue period, the important thing about Jesus is that he was a Jew, a Jew whose ministry was to serve his people. This Jesus, van Buren believes, can be reconstructed from the text. There is an anti-Judaic Jesus in the text too, but this Jesus is a Jesus of the final editing of the text; a Jesus imaged by the early church which does not reflect the historical Jesus.

Van Buren views Jesus as an eschatological prophet standing in the tradition of Jewish restoration theology. But Jesus' apocalyptic perspective does not fit well into van Buren's worldview, so he gives a functional analysis to its language: this language functioned to place the hearer before God in the present.

What Jesus attempted in his lifetime was a renewal movement within Israel; he attempted to get his people to commit themselves anew to the covenant. He effected this renewal, in those in whom he did affect it, by presenting them with the immediacy of God.

For van Buren of the Jewish-Christian dialogue period, the historical Jesus and the Christ of faith function in the same way: Jesus confronted his people with the immediacy of God, and as the Christ of faith he continues to do so.

The difference between Jesus and the Christ of faith is audience. Jesus' ministry was to his people. The Christ of faith functions within the context of the church, and the church is a Gentile church.

For van Buren, the church was meant by God to exist alongside Israel, and to cooperate with Israel and with God for the sake of world redemption. That this is not what happened historically is due to a church error. The anti-Judaic church is not the church that God intended.

God did intend the Gentile church. God's vehicle for creating the church was not Jesus — Jesus' ministry was to his people; he did not intend to found a Gentile church — but Paul. Paul, as van Buren reads him, is not anti-Judaic. Rather, the message of Paul is that Gentiles through their faith in Jesus Christ are included in the covenant that began with Abraham. Indeed, Gentile inclusion through the ministry of Paul is the fulfillment of a promise that God had made to Abraham, namely, that he (Abraham) would be the father of many nations. Just as Israel's story begins with Abraham, so does the story of the church; both together are the story of the covenant.

For van Buren, Easter is a covenantal event that can be described in a way similar to the covenantal event of Sinai. Important to a covenantal event is that the event is initiated by God, but the human response is also constitutive of the event.

Easter is a beginning; it is the beginning of Gentile inclusion in the covenant. Easter is a hope. Because Easter is the event that draws Gentiles into the covenant, Gentiles share the hope of the covenant, and share the responsibility for what is hoped for — world redemption.

Salvation is fully future in the Jewish-Christian reality; and this is to say that world redemption is not a reality, it is a hope. What is a reality is the church existing alongside Israel in a covenant that is not finished, but open to the future.

Chapter Eight

A Theology of the Jewish-Christian Reality: Christianity and Judaism, Other Religions, and Last Things

In this chapter we first consider van Buren's Post-Holocaust theology of the Cross. It involves a familial model of God, which we argue is not satisfying as an explanation of why God acts the way God does in the world; it is especially not satisfying in terms of the Holocaust. In the last chapter, Chapter Seven, we considered how van Buren understood the church to have been incorporated into the covenant. In this chapter we consider his view on how the church, now a member of the covenant, is to (should) relate to its covenantal partner, Israel. The church has a mission to Israel, but it is not that of attempting to convert Israel to Christianity; rather, its mission is to serve Israel. Van Buren has some interesting things to say about how the church should do this. Van Buren's view of the Jewish-Christian reality does make room for other religions. But, while he wishes to dialogue with other religions, his worldview may hinder his ability to do so. The final section of this chapter presents van Buren's picture of the End. It follows from van Buren's worldview that there must be an end. But it also follows from his worldview that there is no necessity for there to be a particular end, no necessity to the end being good.

1. The Holocaust, The Cross, and a Familial Model of the God of the Covenant.

Van Buren's interpretation of the significance of the Cross for the Jewish-Christian reality is an interpretation based on his understanding of the Holocaust — van Buren's theology of the Cross is a Post-Holocaust theology. For this reason we must begin with van Buren's response to the Holocaust.[1]

From a faith perspective the central question in terms of the Holocaust seems to be: Where was God in all of this? Van Buren's answer to this question is: God chose to suffer in solidarity with God's people (van Buren 1980, 117). Why did God choose to act in this way? Van Buren's tentative answer to this is: God chose to allow the Holocaust to happen in order to awaken the church to the error of its anti-Judaic tradition. In other words, van Buren knows that the church (as evident in Post-Holocaust church documents) has repudiated its anti-Judaic tradition, and has affirmed the eternal covenant between God and Israel. And, he knows that it has done so because of the Holocaust, and because of the recognition that the church's anti-Judaic tradition played a role in the Holocaust's happening. Might God then have intended the Holocaust for this purpose, for the purpose of awakening God's church to its error of anti-Judaism? Van Buren first suggests this, but then withdraws it. He withdraws it because the cost seems too high (van Buren 1980, 117). Would God have allowed six million of God's people to have died, in the way in which they did die, in order to correct church teaching? Van Buren would have been better off not even to have made this tentative suggestion. But, besides this, there is something fundamentally wrong with van Buren's suggestion, and that is that it implies that one can speak of the Holocaust in terms of God's purpose in the first place. Just as van Buren learns from Fackenheim to understand Easter not as an accomplished fact, but as a beginning and as a hope, so he also learns from Fackenheim to understand the Holocaust, and therefore also the Cross, in terms other than those of God's purpose or intent. For Fackenheim, "No purpose, religious or non-religious, will ever be found in Auschwitz. The very attempt to find one is blasphemous" (Fackenheim 1978, 27).

Again, for van Buren, God chose to suffer in solidarity with God's people in the Holocaust. Why did God not choose to intervene on God's people's behalf, instead? Van Buren in *A Christian Theology of the People Israel* responds this way:

> No consensus has yet emerged on God's apparent withdrawal from his responsibility to protect his people in their hour of desperate need. How or in what way God abided by the terms of the partnership of the covenant in the Holocaust remains a painful mystery (van Buren 1983, 298-99).

In *Christ in Context* van Buren says that God chose not to rescue God's people in the Holocaust "for reasons of which we cannot be sure" (van Buren 1988, 166). In other words, van Buren seems to respond to the fact that God did not rescue in the Holocaust by saying that we don't know why. But van Buren does not rest content with this "We don't know" position. He goes beyond this position to another position involving a familial model of the God of the covenant (van Buren 1980, 151-53 and 183 and van Buren 1988, 209).

According to van Buren, the God of the covenant wills to be not a dictator nor a sovereign king, but rather a loving father. How does a loving father behave toward his children (God's covenantal partners)? According to van Buren, this way: The father must give his children room to grow. If the father were to do everything for his children, then they would never learn how to do things for themselves. They would never become the responsible adults that the father wants his children to become. He must give them room to grow. This means letting them make mistakes and suffering with them as they painfully learn from their mistakes. For the father to step in and fix the mistakes his children make would not be the loving fatherly thing to do, because then his children would not learn from their mistakes; they would not grow; they would think that no matter what they do, father will fix it. So the father must exercise restraint, even if it is painful for the father to watch while his children suffer because of their mistakes. Still, it is better to suffer with them than to do for them what they should learn to do for themselves. This is van Buren's understanding of the God of the covenant as a loving father (van Buren 1988, 166).

This model of God as a loving father who holds back and does not interfere in our lives in order that we might learn from our mistakes, and therefore grow because of them — this model might help us to explain many painful experiences in which we do not perceive much or any help coming from God, but are able, none the less, to struggle through on our own, and perhaps even learn something in the process. Nevertheless, this model falters as a model for explaining God's behavior in the Holocaust.

If his children fall down, the father might show restraint and let them pick themselves up. After all, there is a lesson in that. And, the father might do this even if the children hurt themselves in the fall, and perhaps are even crying because of the fall. Such a thing hurts the father too, just seeing it happen to his children. So, he may choose not to intervene, but rather to suffer with his children for the sake of the lesson. But what about the case in which the children's lives are threatened? Or, what about the case in which the children are dying? What about the case of the Holocaust? What would be the purpose of fatherly restraint in this case? In this case wouldn't the fatherly thing to do be to save the children?

According to van Buren, God chose to suffer in solidarity with God's people in the Holocaust, rather than to solve their problems for them (van Buren 1988, 166-7). God chose to suffer in solidarity with God's people rather than intervene on their behalf to show that God wants God's creatures to take responsibility for the future of God's creation; indeed, God wants God's covenantal partners to take the lead in restoring what is corrupt in God's creation (van Buren 1988, 167). Van Buren believes that God did not intervene in the Holocaust because God decided not to do for us what God has given us the freedom and responsibility to do for ourselves. And, van Buren believes that God's action here (God's decisions) are consistent with the model of God as a loving parent (van Buren 1980, 117 and van Buren 1988, 167). God may have made the decisions that van Buren says that God made. But we do not agree that these decisions are consistent with God as a loving father. A loving father does not give more responsibility to his children than they can handle. Or, if the father gives his children responsibility that he later learns is too much for them — and for van Buren's model of God this is a possible scenario — then the father withdraws the responsibility. A loving father intervenes when his children are threatened; a loving father intervenes when his children are dying. This does not mean that we think that God is not a God of love, even if logic would force us to this position. Rather, we think that the Holocaust remains a theological problem: Why God did not intervene in the Holocaust is a painful mystery.

For van Buren, the Holocaust changes forever the way he views his own faith, the Christian faith. This is so because the church is implicated in the fact of the Holocaust:

> It surely was not the sufficient cause of the horror, but without it, it is difficult to account for the passivity before the fact, not to speak of actual cooperation with it in all too many cases of so many Christians. (van Buren 1988, 161)

Because the church is implicated in the Holocaust, this has caused the church to repudiate its anti-Judaic past, and to affirm the eternal covenant between God and Israel. But, if this is so, then the church after Auschwitz can no longer take a position that would undercut this new affirmation of the Jewish people. But the traditional (Protestant) doctrine of the Atonement does exactly that, as we saw when we considered van Buren's early theological position under Karl Barth.[2] If, after Auschwitz, this doctrine of the church can no longer be used to understand the significance of the Cross, then how is the Cross to be understood? How is the Cross to be seen in the light of Auschwitz?

If the Holocaust is not to be understood in terms of God's intention, then the Cross is not to be understood in terms of God's intention, either (van Buren 1988, 164). If the Holocaust was a defeat for God and God's cause — the advancement of the covenant and its purpose — then the Cross was a defeat for God and God's cause, too (van Buren 1988, 166).

According to van Buren, God did not intend that Jesus should die on the Cross — his death was a tragic accident (van Buren 1988, 172-3). Nevertheless, God accepted what happened and the disciples' reaction to it as a fresh opportunity for a new contribution toward the renewal of God's creation (van Buren 1988, 172-73).

God did not intend the Cross; nevertheless, God used it and the disciples' reaction to it, to further God's cause. One thing we might note about this notion of van Buren's is that it is consistent with his worldview. God by virtue of God's decision to create the world became a person (the normative person) in space and time, who in covenanting with God's creatures must wait for their response to God's initial act. God does not know ahead of time how they will respond; God has created them free to decide how they will respond. Further, because the future is not determined by God alone but by God and God's covenantal partners — God's intention is for the future to develop covenantally — God does not know the world's (creation's) future ahead of time, either (van Buren 1988, 185). The covenant is like a conversation (van Buren 1983, 103 and 108), or like a game (van Buren 1988, 185), in the sense that once the conversation or game gets started (it is started by God) then each party (God and God's creatures) to the conversation speaks in response to what the other party has said; then each player moves in response to the moves of the other player. Neither party knows what the other party will say; together they create a conversation. Neither player knows the moves of the other player; together they create a game. God and God's covenantal partners together create a covenantal path through history, a path hopefully leading to redemption.

The Cross was a defeat for God. It was a defeat for God because it was a defeat for Jesus. Jesus' ministry was to effect a renewal movement within Israel — to cause his people to renew their commitment to the covenant. This did not happen; instead, Jesus died on the Cross. The Cross was a defeat for Jesus, and therefore a defeat for God; a defeat for God's cause — the advancement of the covenant (van Buren 1988, 167-70). The Holocaust was a defeat of God's cause, and so was the Cross.

A central question of the Holocaust is: where was God? A central question of the Cross is: where was God? In van Buren's early theological career we saw that he went against classical Christology and its view that God does not suffer, because that view was inconsistent with another view that both van Buren and traditional Christianity held, namely, that Jesus Christ is the full and complete revelation of God. In his Jewish-Christian dialogue period, van Buren obviously no longer holds the latter view. Certainly Jesus Christ (the Easter-Pentecost event) remains revelation for van Buren. But now it is revelation for a Gentile church; a revelation that does not supersede the revelation of Sinai. Nevertheless, van Buren continues to believe in a God who suffers; only now he has different reasons for this belief. For van Buren, Auschwitz may teach us what we should have learned at Golgotha: God enters into the pain and suffering of God's children (van Buren 1988, 165).

God did not intend the Holocaust nor the Cross. Responsibility for these events is human responsibility.[3] These events were defeats for

God, defeats for God's cause. In the face of these human events, God chose to suffer with God's children; to suffer with Jesus on the Cross, to suffer even more with God's sons and daughters in the Holocaust (van Buren 1988, 166). The question is, why did God choose this way, and not another? Why did God choose to suffer with Jesus and the Holocaust victims, and not to rescue them? We have already considered van Buren's answer to this question: God chooses not to do for us what God wills that we should do for ourselves. God wishes to give to God's covenantal partners more and more of the responsibility for the course the covenant will take. When we fail or make a mistake, God chooses to suffer with us rather than to fix it for us. God chooses to accomplish God's purpose, which is none other than the purpose of the covenant, by accepting failure where it occurs, and suffering with those who suffer as a consequence of those failures (van Buren 1988, 175).

For van Buren, the Cross was a defeat, a defeat for God's cause. But Easter is a sign that God's cause continues. So the Cross was not a final defeat. The Holocaust was a defeat for God, too. But, for van Buren, the state of Israel and the church's repudiation of its anti-Judaic tradition are signs that the Holocaust was not a final defeat, either (van Buren 1988, 181).

The story of the covenant is not over. Because of the Cross and Easter and the way in which those events were brought to Gentiles by Paul, the church exists. It exists alongside Israel in a covenant with God, the purpose of which is world redemption. If a mistake was made that placed Jews and Christians at odds with one another as to whose covenant it was, as to who are the chosen people of God, as to who is the true Israel, perhaps that mistake is finally being corrected; at least van Buren hopes it is. What God intended was for Christians and Jews to cooperate with one another and with God for the sake of world redemption, for the sake of the covenant's purpose. If Christians and Jews were finally to cooperate, they would be cooperating in a covenant that moves through history without guarantees; there is no sure and certain hope that the covenant will end with world redemption. Still, there is hope that it might. The story of the covenant is not over (van Buren, 1988, 180-82).

2. The Church's Mission to Israel.

The church is a community of believers called out of many nations into the covenant with God through faith in Jesus Christ to exist alongside Israel and to cooperate with Israel and with God for the sake of the covenant's purpose, the redemption of the world. The church's mission to the world is to continuously draw people into the church, into the covenant with God through faith in Jesus Christ (van Buren 1983, 320-22 and 332).. This is not, however, the extent of the church's mission to the world, as we shall see when we cover van Buren's view on the Jewish-Christian reality and other religions; this we do in the next section. But the church also has a mission to Israel, and this is the subject of the present section.

Van Buren's position is that the church should serve Israel. His argument for this position is as follows: The church has throughout its history followed an anti-Judaic Jesus. But, as we have seen, an anti-Judaic Jesus was a product of the early church which was in conflict with Judaism and projected that conflict onto Jesus, while Jesus himself was in solidarity with his people. Jesus was a Jew who served his people. Van Buren's favorite biblical passage to cite in support of his view here is Roman 15:8, "For I tell you that Christ became a servant to the circumcised to show God's truthfulness, in order to confirm the promises given to the patriarchs." But if Jesus served his people, and Jesus both then and now is to be understood in the context of Israel, then Jesus' followers both then and now are to serve Israel too, for they are in that same context.[4] The church's mission to Israel is to serve Israel, just as its Lord served Israel (van Buren 1988, 77-78).
But if the church's mission to Israel is to serve Israel, what service is it to perform?

Jesus' ministry was to effect a renewal movement within Israel; his purpose was to help Israel to be what it was called to be, namely Israel, a people called into a covenant with God. Van Buren suggests that Jesus' ministry to Israel should also be the church's ministry to Israel (van Buren 1983, 333). Although van Buren immediately recognizes that it is somewhat presumptuous of a Gentile church to think that it can have a role in Israel's task of being true to its calling and being Israel, he, nevertheless, suggests that the church can serve Israel in this way. The church can help Israel be Israel by acknowledging and witnessing to the world to Israel's election. In other words, what van

Buren is suggesting is that the church should and can serve Israel by acknowledging what is for van Buren the very premise on which his theology of the Jewish-Christian reality is itself based; namely, the eternal covenant between God and Israel. The church can serve Israel, and can help Israel to be Israel by witnessing to the world Israel's election (van Buren 1983, 334).

The church has been for most of its existence a church with an anti-Judaic tradition. Anti-Judaism is a term within a theological discourse. It translates on a sociological level as anti-semitism. The church is responsible for much of the hatred shown the Jewish people, and the ultimate consequences of that hatred — the death of many Jews. Van Buren suggests that a church that wishes to make amends for its anti-Judaic past, and a church that wishes to serve Israel and to see itself as called by God to serve Israel, will be a church that sees as its mission that of being the Anti-Defamation League of the Jewish people. The church that for most of its history attacked and persecuted Israel, now, in a Post-Holocaust world in which it has become aware of its anti-Judaic error and its call to serve Israel, will make amends for its error and will serve Israel by being its protector and its defender (van Buren 1983, 335-6).

In his presentation on how the church might serve Israel, van Buren has some interesting things to say about intermarriage between Christians and Jews, and about how the church might respond to Jews who seriously "convert" to Christianity. Should one of the parties to an intermarriage between a Jew and a Christian convert to the religion of the other — the Jew convert to Christianity, or the Christian convert to Judaism? Van Buren favors neither party converting to the other religion. Rather, he feels the frontiers of a new beginning in the relationship between Christians and Jews living together the covenant with God might be explored in such a setting — in the setting of a marriage. But the question then becomes, what if the marriage produces children, how are they to be raised, as Christians or as Jews? Van Buren responds to this question this way: Because of the relative numbers of the church and the Jewish people, the "loss" to the church, if it is decided to raise the children as Jews, is as nothing when compared to the gain for Israel (van Buren 1983, 340).

Van Buren does not encourage Jews converting to Christianity. From his point of view, there is no need for such conversion: both Christians and Jews are parties to the one covenant with God.

Nevertheless, van Buren recognizes that some Jews do "convert" to Christianity. The question is, what should be their status within the church? Van Buren suggests this: They should remain faithful to Torah, and thus, be among Gentile Christians as a living sign of the people on whose election that of the Gentile church depends — without Israel as its context, the church would not exist (van Buren 1983, 340). Suppose a Jew wanted to worship with Christians. Would such a Jew be excluded from the Eucharist? For a Christian baptism is a requirement for receiving communion. Must this also be a requirement for a Jew who wishes to worship with Christians? Van Buren says, No. His reason is that the church has made baptism an unambiguous sign for Jews of their departure from their people and a renunciation of the covenant. Jews should be able to share in the celebration of the Holy Eucharist as Jews (van Buren 1983, 341).

Van Buren views all of his suggestions on how the church might serve Israel as simply that, suggestions. His intent is to stimulate discussion on how the church might turn itself around from negating and persecuting Israel to serving Israel. His hope is that a church that understands that to follow its Lord is to follow its Lord in serving Israel, and acts on that understanding, will also cause Israel to no longer see the church as the enemy, but as a partner. Van Buren has the further hope that Jews and Christians might become mutually supportive partners in a covenant they share with one another and with God (van Buren 1983, 351).

3. The Jewish-Christian Reality and Other Religions.

Van Buren has written a three volume set on the Jewish-Christian reality — *Discerning the Way, A Christian Theology of the People Israel, Christ in Context* — and we have been considering these volumes in our desire to understand and to assess van Buren's contribution to the Jewish-Christian dialogue. Van Buren intends to write a fourth volume in which he will address the issue of the Jewish-Christian reality and other religions (van Buren 1983, 326). Nevertheless, even in the volumes that van Buren has written we can get an idea how his views in this area might develop.

In van Buren's early theological period under Barth we saw that like Barth van Buren was Christocentric. What this means is that van Buren saw everything from a Christocentric perspective: Jesus Christ is the full and complete revelation of God. From this perspective there is no room for Judaism, nor for any other religion for that matter. We might call this period van Buren's exclusivistic period — Christianity is the only true religion.

In *The Secular Meaning of the Gospel* van Buren gave some validity to other religions. Each religion could acknowledge validity in another religion when it saw in it the same thing that gave validity to its own religion; for van Buren that same thing was freedom. Nevertheless, the source of that validity was not attributed to whatever the religion in question said was its source; rather, the source was attributed to that which gave validity to one's own religion; for Christianity that would be Jesus. In other words, for Christians Jesus is the source of freedom regardless of which religious context freedom is found. If a Hindu exhibited freedom, a Christian would say it is because of Jesus. Of course, for van Buren, the same thing is true for all other religions: each might give validity to other religions, but each would do so in terms of its own religion, not in terms of those other religions, not in terms of what other religions would say gave validity to themselves. This is an inclusivist view: one sees in other religions the same thing that validates one's own religion. A Christian, for example, sees in other religions what those other religions cannot see in themselves, namely, Jesus Christ. Jesus Christ gives validity to all religions, even if it is only a Christian who knows that, or rather would say that. Any other religion would claim that it is what validates its own religion that also validates all others.

In the Jewish-Christian dialogue period van Buren becomes a religious pluralist (van Buren 1988, 194-5). For van Buren in this period, the church has been given a way by God, and Israel has been given a way by God; the two have been given different ways in the one covenant. If this is so, the question might be put: Has God given other ways, as well, to others not the church and not Israel? Van Buren's answer to this question is, if this is so, it has not been revealed to the church nor to Israel. What has been revealed to the church and to Israel is what validates them, their own story. But their story says nothing about the story of others, nor even that others have their own story (van Buren 1980, 136 and 167; van Buren 1983, 142; van Buren 1988, 85 and 93). Van Buren's answer to our question is, the church does not know: "What the church does not know is whether and how others may have found themselves, apart from Jesus and Israel, present to God" (van Buren 1988, 93). That the church does not know the answer to this question, does not mean for van Buren that the church cannot come to know the answer to it: "It would seem wise for the church at least to be open and receptive to the possibility that there may be many ways in which men and women can be and are present to God..." (van Buren 1988, 93).

The question now becomes this: If Christians do not know if God has given other ways to other people, but should remain open and receptive to the possibility, how would they come to know whether this is true? Van Buren's answer to this question is this: First, in order to be receptive and open to the possibility that God may have given other ways to other people, the church should "abandon its earlier dreams of being a world-church, and accept its particularity as a minority in God's World" (van Buren 1983, 175). To do this is to place the church in a position to know how God has given other ways to other people. Then the church actually comes to know these other ways by entering into dialogue with other religions; Christians tell their story and allow others to tell their's (van Buren 1983, 175).

The limit to van Buren's openness to other religions would seem to be his worldview:

> Israel, alive to this day, stands in its peoplehood as an invitation to the nation of Islam, the Hindu nation, the native American nations, and to all the rest, to see in their own peoplehood the hand of the Creator of heaven and earth, who through the cooperation of his creatures means to preserve and move toward completion his beloved creation (van Buren 1983, 175).[5]

Would van Buren's position be able to tolerate a story that did not include language of a personal God, the "Creator of heaven and earth"? Could it tolerate a story that did not include the term "covenant," nor viewed reality as history moving in one direction? Could it tolerate a story in which salvation was not understood as a future possibility for creation, but rather understood salvation in completely different terms? Could van Buren's position tolerate a religion that did not formulate itself in terms of a story at all? Van Buren's worldview may limit his ability to dialogue with other religions.

4. A Theology of the Jewish-Christian Reality and the Language of Nicea and Chalcedon.

In van Buren's early theology he criticized classical Christology for being inconsistent: it affirmed the full and complete revelation of Jesus Christ, on the one hand, but assumed that God could not suffer (change), on the other. Van Buren, wishing to be more consistent, affirmed the first — Jesus Christ is the full and complete revelation of God — and denied the second — God could not suffer; indeed, God suffered on the Cross. In *The Secular Meaning of the Gospel* there is no room for talk of God, so no room for talk of a God who suffers, either. In his secular period, van Buren's criticism of classical Christology was that it does not do justice to Jesus' humanity. In the Jewish-Christian dialogue period, van Buren returns to God-talk and returns to the notion that God suffers, although for different reasons than the reasons of his early theological period. In the Jewish-Christian dialogue period, God is capable of suffering (changing) by virtue of God's decision to create. God in fact suffers because God would rather suffer with us in our failures than to do for us what God wills that we do for ourselves. In van Buren's Jewish-Christian dialogue period, his criticism of classical Christology is that it completely ignores covenantal theology, God as God of the covenant; it completely ignores Jesus as a Jew, Jesus in the context of Israel (van Buren 1988, 215-16).

In van Buren's early theological period, he accepted classical Christology except for the belief that God could not suffer. In van Buren's secular period, he gave a "call" and "response" christology which viewed Jesus Christ functionally, and not ontologically. In his Jewish-Christian dialogue period, van Buren returns to his "call" and "response" Christology of his secular period, but with some differences; for example, there is no exclusivistic language in van Buren's "call" and "response" Christology of his Jewish-Christian dialogue period. What is the same is that Jesus is viewed functionally and not ontologically. Jesus is viewed as a man, but now more specifically, more contextually. Jesus is viewed as a Jew. Jesus was a Jew called by God to play a role in bringing Jews back to the God of the covenant, and, as Lord of the church, in bringing Gentiles into the covenant (van Buren 1988, 225-6, 229, and 253).

In *The Secular Meaning of the Gospel*, while van Buren was critical of classical Christology, he still felt the need to interpret his secular Christianity in terms of its language. In his Jewish-Christian dialogue period, van Buren feels the same need: he interprets his theology of the Jewish-Christian reality in terms of the language of classical Christology. To give but one example: In classical Christology the two natures of the Son are inseparably and indivisibly united. What this means in terms of van Buren's Jewish-Christian reality is first that God and Israel are inseparable and indivisible in the context of the covenant. But secondly, because Jesus was a Jew and therefore a part of Israel, this also means that he, the Jew Jesus, and the God of Israel are inseparable and indivisible in the context of the same covenant (van Buren 1988, 255-6). Again, we think such an interpretation is forced, and we wonder what is gained by it. If you empty the meaning of a doctrine's language, and replace it with meaning in accord with your own view, so that you keep the language but not its meaning, we wonder what has been gained. For van Buren, at any rate, such a task fulfills the responsibility theologians have to interpret their view in terms of the classical tradition. This sense of responsibility van Buren inherited from Karl Barth.

5. Last Things.

God decided to create. God's initial act of Creation though was but a beginning. This was so because even in that initial act God had decided that what God had begun, would only reach completion when God's creatures cooperated with God in bringing it about. What Israel knows and what the church knows is how God has drawn them into this cooperation for the sake of world redemption; what they know is their own story, the story of the covenant. But God may have dealt with others, and may have intended to deal with others, in ways other than through the covenant known by Israel and the church. The way in which Israel and the church may come to know whether this is so, is to dialogue with other religious traditions. In any event, what God is about is attempting to draw all of God's creatures into a cooperative effort with God for the sake of completing what God alone had but begun — God solicits our help in the creative process that has as its goal world redemption. Our final question is this: If God finally was able to gain the cooperation of all God's creatures, if the purpose of the covenant found its fulfillment, if the movement of history reached its intended end, if world redemption were to occur, what would it look like?

First, we might mention again that in van Buren's worldview there is no necessity that history end with world redemption. There is in van Buren's worldview the necessity of an end; creation does not go on forever; it is not eternal. But there is no necessity that it end well. This separates van Buren's worldview from worldviews that are similar to his (Rosenzweig's and Greenberg's, for example). There is nothing inevitable about the world ending well. If it were to end well that would be because God's creatures turned to God in the spirit of cooperation. But there is no necessity to this, and so no necessity to the world ending well, either. The end may not be world redemption. In the end there may be only God, not God and creation at all (van Buren 1988, 287-8, and 296). But if this were so, it would be a failed end, not the end that God intended. Will God alone without creation in fact be the end? We do not know; God does not know; no one knows (van Buren 1988, 287)..

If we do not know what the end will be, still we can try to imagine what the end would be if it turned out to be world redemption. Van Buren gives two pictures.

Van Buren's vision of the end is an attempt to interpret 1 Cor. 15:28, "When all things are subjected to him [i.e., the Son], then the Son himself will be subjected to him [i.e., the Father] who put all things under him, that God may be all in all" (van Buren 1988, 284). The question for van Buren is: What does it mean that God may be all in all? What does "all in all" mean?

First, we might mention that for van Buren (and for Paul), the end is theocentric. The church is Christocentric but this is only temporally true. In the end Christ lays down his role of bringing Christians before God (van Buren 1988, 106). For van Buren, it is also true that the role that Torah plays for Israel is set aside with world redemption (van Buren 1983, 231). One thing that God is all in all means is that Christ and Torah no longer function the way they did before world redemption; a redeemed world is a theocentric world.

Van Buren's first picture of world redemption is a picture in which God is passively at the center, and all God's creatures are actively serving God (van Buren 1988, 285). But this picture seems not to satisfy van Buren, since he gives a second picture in which God is more active:

> The goal of God the Father may therefore be the free reign of all his goodness, his graciousness and mercy, his self-giving for the well-being of his whole creation. In the end, God's goal may prove to be his full sharing of all he is and has with all his creatures, thus becoming everything to everyone. (van Buren 1988, 298)

This is a picture in which God is more active than in the first picture van Buren paints. But, still it is not a clear picture. What would a picture look like that had God "sharing all he is and has with all his creatures"? Van Buren's picture in fact gives very little detail; he leaves the picture vague. Perhaps he is aware of this when he says: "Perhaps no human vision of the end of the story into which the church has been grafted can or need count for much" (van Buren 1988, 299). Still, van Buren might have let his imagination run wild here. His Jewish-Christian reality is a this-world reality; heaven exists, if it exists at all in this view, as this world when it reaches redemption, if it ever does. Van Buren might have painted a picture of a world infinitely better than the one we in fact live in. He might have painted a picture of a world hoped for; a world as it ought to be; a world as it could be if we would but turn to God in a spirit of cooperation. Instead, the picture is left vague, and we wonder why. After all, van Buren's picture of reality places all value in this world. If we have a future at all, it is in this world. The purpose of our lives is to do all we can to advance the world toward its completion. Our future, if we have a future, depends on the world being redeemed. When we die our ability to help the advancement is ended; the future of the living and the dead is in the hands of the living. It seems to us the purpose of all of this, the purpose of placing all value in the only reality we know, the reality of this world, is to motivate us to do all we can while we are alive to work for our future and everyone's future, including God's future. It seems to us that a picture here of what we are working towards, a picture of the way things could be, even if such a picture is simply the exercise of the imagination, could be helpful. It could further motivate us to do all we can to advance the only reality we know, the only reality there is.

Chapter Nine

An Assessment of van Buren's Theology of the Jewish-Christian Reality

In this the final chapter we assess the contribution of van Buren's "A Theology of the Jewish-Christian reality" to the Jewish-Christian dialogue. We organize our assessment around these questions: Would Christians recognize themselves as characterized in van Buren's theology? Would Christians accept the way they are characterized in van Buren's theology? Would Jews recognize or accept the way they are characterized in van Buren's theology? Because we argue that there is good reason to believe that van Buren's one covenant theory would not be acceptable to the dialogue participants, particularly the Jewish participants, we develop an alternative to van Buren's one covenant view. We call it an overlapping view of the two faiths, and we suggest it as our own attempt at making a contribution to the Jewish-Christian dialogue. While van Buren understands Torah and Jesus Christ as functioning in similar if not identical ways in Judaism and Christianity respectively, he never attempts to relate them. Indeed, the attempt to relate them is lacking in the Jewish-Christian dialogue itself. As a further attempt at a contribution we suggest a way of understanding the relationship of the two central symbols of Judaism and Christianity.

1. Van Buren's "A Theology of the Jewish-Christian Reality" viewed from the Christian side.

Would Christians recognize themselves as characterized by van Buren's theology? Van Buren is attempting to make a contribution to the Jewish-Christian dialogue. The premise on which his theology rests is that the church now in the 20th century confesses that the covenant between God and Israel is eternal. For the church to make such a confession, for the church to recognize and acknowledge the validity of Judaism, is for the church to reverse its teaching on Judaism, a teaching that it has held for most if not all of its history. Van Buren is not claiming that the church has in fact made this confession, and understands the implication of this confession. But rather he is claiming that there is evidence in contemporary church documents that the church is beginning to make this confession, and is beginning to understand what this confession means for the church. Such a confession by the church, or even the beginning of this confession by the church — the reversal of its teaching on Judaism and the repudiation of its anti-Judaic tradition — is an incredible event in the life of the church, an event perhaps unequaled in the church's life. This is so because this confession throws into question the very definition of the church. The church had claimed as its own validity that which had been Israel's. With the coming of Christ the church displaced Israel. The church indeed was the true Israel, or so the church claimed. But, if the church returns the validity to Israel that it had for most of its history denied was Israel's but rather its own, then it leaves itself without any validity of its own. The church's anti-Judaic tradition was a principal means by which it affirmed and defined itself. For the church to confess that the covenant between God and Israel is eternal, is also to recognize that the church needs to redefine itself. Van Buren's theology is just such an undertaking. It attempts a redefinition of Christianity; it attempts to draw a Christianity that does not repudiate Judaism in its desire to affirm itself, but rather affirms Judaism in its desire to affirm itself. Would Christians recognize themselves as characterized by van Buren's theology? Our first response to this question would have to be this: Christians, in order even to consider van Buren's theology, must accept his basic premise, namely, that the church acknowledge the eternal covenant between God and Israel; and, because of this acknowledgement, must be open to understanding itself in new ways, particularly in ways that make room for the validity of Judaism. Christians who will not go this far with van Buren obviously will not find van Buren's theology acceptable, will not recognize themselves as characterized by van Buren's theology. Christians who might find van Buren's theology acceptable, who would at least consider his view, are Christians open to the Jewish-Christian dialogue.

John Pawlikowski, a participant in the Jewish-Christian dialogue, has considered van Buren's reformulated view of Christianity and finds it unacceptable. He calls van Buren's view of Christianity, Christianity as Judaism for Gentiles (Pawlikowski 1982, 3). Pawlikowski did not have the advantage of reviewing van Buren's position as it is found in *A Christian Theology of the People Israel,* and *Christ in Context*; his assessment of van Buren came before these two books were published. So we might ask this question: From the vantage point of van Buren's later work, is Pawlikowski's characterization of van Buren's view of Christianity valid? Is van Buren's view of Christianity simply Judaism for Gentiles? For van Buren, Torah is a door into the covenant for Jews, and Jesus Christ is a door into that same covenant for Christians. But the covenant itself is formulated within Judaism. So, aren't Christians simply Gentiles entering into Judaism by a different door?

Although van Buren maintains a one covenant theory, much of what he has to say about Judaism and Christianity would be more at home in a two covenant theory. It is because of this that we feel van Buren can be defended against the charge that he presents a Christianity that is simply Judaism for Gentiles.[1]

In many ways van Buren presents Judaism and Christianity as autonomous but equally valid religions. But these are features of a two covenant theory, at least as such a theory is presented by the participants to the Jewish-Christian dialogue that we have considered: Martin Buber, Hans Joahim Schoeps, and Rosemary Ruether.

The two faith communities rest on different foundations: Sinai is foundational for Israel; Jesus Christ is foundational for the church (van Buren 1988, 211 and 260). Indeed, much of what makes Judaism and Christianity different is their different central symbols, although these different symbols function in similar if not identical ways: The vehicle of revelation for Israel is Torah; the vehicle of revelation for the church is Jesus Christ (van Buren 1983, 7). Expressed in a different way: The way in which God is present to Israel is Torah, the way in which God is present to the church is Jesus Christ (van Buren 1988, 251). The path, the way into history for Israel, is Torah; the path, the way into history for the church is Jesus Christ (van Buren 1983, 7 and 159).

The life of the community is shaped by Torah for Israel; the life of the Christian community is shaped by Jesus Christ (van Buren 1983, 157 and 239). God unveils God's love for Israel in Torah, and God's love for the church in Jesus Christ (van Buren 1983, 29). Judaism and Christianity are autonomous in the sense that they rest on different foundations: Torah for Israel, Jesus Christ for the church.

If in some sense Judaism and Christianity are autonomous religions for van Buren, they are for him also equally valid. The church is in as intimate a relationship with God as Israel. In terms of nearness and intimacy with God, the two faith communities are equal (van Buren 1983, 236, and van Buren 1988, 1445). For van Buren, the Exodus/Sinai event and the Easter/Pentecost event were pro-toredemptive, and both communities in their worship services experience, or can experience a foretaste of that redemption still awaited (van Buren 1983, 69-70 and van Buren 1988, 255). In many ways for van Buren Judaism and Christianity are autonomous and equally valid vehicles of salvation; and, again, these are features of a two covenant theory.

Our first response to the charge that van Buren's theology presents Christianity as Judaism for Gentiles is this: Van Buren presents Judaism and Christianity in many ways as two autonomous and equally valid religious communities existing alongside one another, and in van Buren's presentation the Christian community is defined and its life is shaped in terms that are Christian. Even if Christians are included in the same covenant as Israel, their inclusion is on different terms than that of Israel, terms that are Christian.

A criticism of van Buren's *The Secular Meaning of the Gospel* was that it gave up too much of Christianity to secularism. Another way of expressing the criticism that van Buren, in his Jewish-Christian dialogue period, paints Christianity as simply Judaism for Gentiles, is to say that van Buren gives up too much of Christianity to Judaism.

It is clear that van Buren in reformulating Christianity vis-a-vis Judaism has done so by moving Christianity closer to Judaism. He has argued that the articulation of Christianity without a regard for Judaism, outside the context of Israel, was a mistake, a mistake of the church's anti-Judaic tradition. In moving Christianity back into a Jewish context, van Buren paints a picture of Christianity in which much of what was developed outside of that context does not find a place. For example, the doctrines of the Incarnation, the Atonement, and the Trinity are not found in van Buren's view of Christianity in the Jewish-Christian reality. These are Christian doctrines that Judaism has long rejected. Isn't giving them up a concession to Judaism; and, indeed, too much of a concession? Perhaps; but one could argue that these doctrines cohere and lead to exclusivism, and would have to be given up, or reformulated (which is the tactic van Buren takes) in any event, if Christianity is to be formulated in such a way that makes room for other religions, and specifically, makes room for Judaism. We would argue that Christians who could not recognize themselves in an articulation of Christianity in which these doctrines were not to be found, would be Christians who would not give van Buren his major premise; namely, that the covenant between God and Israel is eternal. Such Christians would not be open to the Jewish-Christian dialogue; at least when the purpose of the dialogue is understood to be that of finding ways of articulating the two faiths that make room for each other; and perhaps even of finding ways of articulating the two faiths so that participants could recognize themselves in such an articulation, could accept the way they were characterized in such an articulation.

What about van Buren's worldview? Would Christians recognize van Buren's worldview as being Christian? There seems to us to be at least two things important to consider in answering this question: (1) the element of risk in the covenantal enterprise, and (2) the this-world nature of Christianity entailed by van Buren's worldview.

Van Buren wrote an article called "William James and Metaphysical Risk" in 1968 during his analytic philosophy of religion period. Nevertheless, the work he did on James during that period carried over into his work in the Jewish-Christian dialogue. Indeed, it is not too much of an exaggeration to say that van Buren's worldview in his theology of the Jewish-Christian reality is in important respects a Jamesian worldview. We believe that van Buren's worldview is more influenced by James than by any Jewish voices he might have listen to in formulating it.

The world as unfinished, God as a limited agent within the world, and God having need of our cooperation if the world is to be made better and reach completion, are all elements of van Buren's worldview that can be found in James (van Buren 1968, 144-6). But perhaps the greatest influence of James on van Buren is in the notion that the covenant cuts a path through history without guarantees. In other words, there is an element of risk in the whole enterprise; world redemption may not be reached. According to van Buren James viewed the world as open-ended, dangerous and venturesome; and he (James) liked it that way(van Buren 1968, 141). James thought that the element of risk in life gave life a high flavor (van Buren 1968, 141), and van Buren agrees with James on this point (van Buren 1968, 241).

But, of course, one can have a different response to the risk and dangers of life. Risk can be a source of anxiety, and one can look to religion for some relief, some assurance.that in spite of everything God will make things turn out right in the end. Van Buren's worldview is similar to Greenberg's and Rosenzweig's. But for these two Jewish thinkers there is some assurance of the final outcome of things: Greenberg views the covenant's advancement towards its goal as being assured.[2] Rosenzweig understood world redemption as inevitable; God will bring it about.[3] We would argue that this message — God will make things turn out right in the end — is essential to both Christianity and Judaism. In so far as van Buren's theology of the Jewish-Christian reality lacks this essential feature, we believe that Christians and Jews will not accept his view of things.

Would Christians recognize themselves as depicted in van Buren's this-world Christianity? Traditional Christianity internalized, spiritualized and personalized salvation. Salvation was accomplished for us by Christ. When Christians die they (their souls) go to heaven where there is eternal life with God. But for van Buren as well as other participants in the Jewish-Christian dialogue (for example, Rosemary Ruether), this teaching was a mistake, a mistake that developed once Christianity had moved out of the context of Israel. For van Buren's this-world Christianity redemption is fully future and is a condition of the world; it is not a condition of individuals. Easter is a beginning (the beginning of the church) and a hope (hope of world redemption). Would Christians recognize themselves in van Buren's this-world Christianity? Again, it depends on whether they are open to viewing themselves in new ways; it depends on whether they are open to the Jewish-Christian dialogue.

Van Buren's view of creation (reality) is that it was not made perfect, and then became corrupt because of "the Fall." Rather, creation was but a beginning. Its completion (redemption) will be accomplished by God and God's creatures working together covenantally towards this end. We have already argued that van Buren's view that there is no guarantee that the process will reach completion, that world redemption will occur, is unacceptable for a Christian view of things. The question now is, would Christians accept that reality, all the reality there is, is this-world?

First let us address the question in terms of an after-life. If an after-life is assured, i.e. world redemption will be reached, then the difference between a this-world Christianity and an other-world Christianity in terms of an after-life would seem to be in when the after-life occurs. For other-world Christianity it is at the time of the person's death. For this-world Christianity it is with the redemption of the world. We do not believe that the difference is so great that it would prevent other-world Christians from considering a this-world perspective, and perhaps even accepting such a perspective. The question is, are there compelling reasons for accepting such a perspective?

God created the world unfinished. God decided that the world would reach completion, perfection, redemption only with the cooperation of God's creatures in a covenantal relationship with one another and with God. The way in which we fulfill our role in this partnership, however limited our role might be, is chiefly through our acts of loving kindness. It is compelling to think that these acts are the stuff of which the world is being made, and the stuff by which the world will reach completion. It is compelling to think that what we do in the world in partnership with God plays a necessary role in creating what we all long for, a redeemed world.

We have said that van Buren's view has many features that are more at home in a two covenant theory than in a one covenant theory. Nevertheless, van Buren maintains a one covenant theory. Van Buren's one covenant theory is based on an interpretation of Paul, a radically new interpretation that views Paul as expressing not a supersessionistic view of Christianity, but rather a view that understands Gentiles through their faith in Jesus Christ as being included in the covenant with Israel. Would Christians recognize themselves in van Buren's one covenant theory? Would they accept themselves as characterized by van Buren's one covenant theory?

Traditionally Christianity has understood its validity as a validity that was passed to it from Judaism. The validity that Judaism had, the church now has. It was taken from Israel by God and given to the church. The church continues a covenant that got started with Israel, but was taken over by the church with the coming of Christ. Or, it can be said a different way: Judaism's validity ends where Christianity's validity begins. The "old" covenant ends where the "new" covenant begins, which is with the coming of Christ. Van Buren's one covenant theory would require Christians to confess not that they have replaced the Jewish people as the chosen people of God, but rather that they too are now, along with the Jewish people, God's chosen people. The covenant is not exclusively the church's, rather God had decided to include the church in a covenant God had long had exclusively with Israel. Would Christians accept this? Would Christians accept that they are not the exclusive members of the covenant with God, but rather were given membership on new terms, the new terms of faith in Jesus Christ, in a covenant that was and is Israel's?

Van Buren would move the church from viewing itself as being in possession of a "new" covenant, to viewing itself as being included in a covenant that did not get started with the church, and had members — the Jewish people — before its own membership. Van Buren would ask the church to view itself as sharing the one covenant. Its validity is a shared validity; the church enters into a validity that is Israel's. Would Christians accept this? We believe that it would be easier for Christians to accept this than Jews.

We have said that for the church to acknowledge the eternal covenant between God and Israel, is also for the church to acknowledge that it needs to reformulate its self-understanding. We have also said that in defining itself, the church cannot help but refer to Judaism. The traditional church's reference to Judaism was its anti-Judaic tradition. Judaism has always rejected this reference to itself. Van Buren's reformulation of Christianity also refers to Judaism. But, as we shall show, at least in terms of van Buren's one covenant theory, we believe that Judaism would also reject van Buren's reformulation of Christianity vis-a-vis Judaism; we believe that Judaism would also reject Christianity's reference to Judaism in van Buren's reformulated view. The problem is van Buren's one covenant theory. We believe that Judaism would reject it. But if one side to the Jewish-Christian dialogue rejects the theory, then it would not be helpful even if the other side were to accept it.

2. Van Buren's "A Theology of the Jewish-Christian Reality" viewed from the Jewish side.

> Christians...are usually very perplexed if one responds truthfully to their question: 'What does Judaism think about Jesus?' with the answer: 'Nothing'
>
> — Franz Rosenzweig

We are not Jewish, so our contribution here is to what we think a response to van Buren's theology of the Jewish-Christian reality might be.[4] Clearly there is much that van Buren has to say about Judaism that would be applauded by Jews, applauded because much of what van Buren has to say is positive, and it is being said by a Christian. For most if not all of its history, Christianity has had only negative things to say about Judaism. Certainly van Buren's main premise — the covenant between God and Israel is eternal — would be applauded by Jews, or at least some Jews, those that would not be uncomfortable with van Buren's emphasis on Israel's divine election. As we have seen, van Buren puts great stress on Israel being defined by its election, and Torah observance as the means by which Jews are sustained in the covenant. Perhaps what van Buren has to say about Judaism would be more warmly received by conservative Jews than by liberal Jews.

It is our belief that Jews would have less trouble with what van Buren has to say about Judaism per se, than they would have with the way in which van Buren reformulates Christianity vis-a-vis Judaism. The traditional church referred to Judaism in a negative way. Christianity of the Jewish-Christian reality does not refer to Judaism in a negative way; nevertheless, the way in which it does refer to Judaism, we feel, would not be accepted by Jews. Again, the problem is with van Buren's one covenant theory.

We have said that while van Buren's view has features that are more at home in a two covenant theory, nevertheless, he maintains a one covenant theory. But, if many of the features of van Buren's view suggests a two covenant theory, then on the basis of what does van Buren maintain a one covenant theory? Even though there exist within the covenant two different communities whose membership in the covenant is on terms also different one from the other, it seems to us that van Buren views the covenant as one because it tells one story, a story that begins with Abraham. For van Buren, there is one story but two different communities, the Jewish community and the Christian community. But now the question is this: How does the story get told?

The church's entry into the covenant, its entrance into the story that began with Abraham, is Jesus; the Gentile church hears from Jesus God's invitation into Israel's story (van Buren 1988, 5, 118, and 278-9). For van Buren the story of Jesus and the story of the church is a new chapter in the story of Israel (van Buren 1983, 320-22, and 352). The church tells Israel's story, and then adds a new chapter to it, the story of Jesus and the story of the church. At this point a Jewish response might be this: First, the church telling Israel's story by listening to Jewish voices to that story, as van Buren seems to want to do, is not something that Jews would be opposed to per se. What one needs to remember is that there is a big difference between a religious community telling its story and another religious community telling it; there is a difference between Israel telling its story, and the church telling Israel's story. Secondly, if the church wishes to add to Israel's story, its own story, a "chapter" that addresses the church, a story the church tells, this too is not something that Jews would be opposed to per se.

The question is: Does the inclusion of the Christian into the story of Israel have implication for Israel? It is clearly true that Judaism has implications for Christianity; without Judaism Christianity never would have come to exist. But is the reverse also true? Does Christianity have implications for Judaism, important theological implications? For van Buren at any rate, Christianity has profound implications for Judaism. The Christian story and Israel's story are one story. This does not mean that Israel tells its story, then the church adds to it its own story, and together, with each community telling its own part, one story is told. For van Buren one story (one covenant) means either party to the story, either religious community must (should) tell the whole story, the one story. In other words, for van Buren, the Christian story is (should be) part of Israel's witness, is (should be) within the testimony of Israel (van Buren 1983, 144-45, and 148). Israel in telling its story must tell the Christian story, and must tell it as a part of its own story. The relationship between Judaism and Christianity is symmetrical in van Buren's one covenant view of them. But would this be acceptable to Jews?

Van Buren's one covenant theory requires Christian affirmation by Jews. It is not an affirmation that would require Jews to deny their own Jewishness, to turn their backs on their Jewish tradition; this was the requirement of the anti-Judaic church. Van Buren's theory would require Jews to affirm Christianity by acknowledging it as a part of their own tradition, a part of their own story. Would Jews accept this?

Van Buren wants Jews to accept the Christian message. This is something the church has always sought from Jews. Traditionally, the church has sought Jewish acceptance of its message by attempting to convert Jews to Christianity. Perhaps, because the church had little success in doing this, it maintained its belief that the Jews would be converted, that the Jews finally would accept the Christian message, by believing that the conversion of the Jews would come just before the End (the Eschaton). Van Buren wants Jews to accept the Christian message, too. But he wants Jews to accept the Christian message not by converting to Christianity, but by accepting the Christian message as part of their own testimony. The church had used its anti-Judaic tradition as a means of self-affirmation and self-definition. Van Buren's one covenant theory requires Israel to accept the church as a part of its self-definition; God has drawn Christians into Israel's story. But, would Jews accept the notion that the Christian story is a story that is a part of its own story, is a part of the story of the Jewish people, is a part of the story Jews tell in order to define who they are? The issue is one of identity; Israel's story is a story of self-definition. Van Buren's one covenant theory threatens Jewish identity. We have no reason to believe that the Jewish community will accept van Buren's one covenant theory.

Again, van Buren developed his theory based on the new interpretation of Paul. This interpretation understands Paul to be claiming that what God was doing through the gospel was drawing Gentiles into the covenant. Paul's view was not an anti-Judaic displacement view, says the new interpretation, but rather a Gentile-inclusion view. Perhaps Paul was saying this. But if so, he never spelled out what the relationship should be, he never explained how the unity of Jews and Gentile Christians was to show itself, and that for the very good reason (so Paul believed) that everything was going to come to an end very soon anyway; indeed, Paul believed the end would come in his own lifetime (1 Thessalonians 4:15-17). But the world did not come to an end, and the church and Israel have existed for over 1900 years in an antagonistic relationship to each other. To now suggest that the two communities identify with one another surely is asking too much. Paul's inclusion-view just does not seem appropriate today as a way of viewing the relationship between Christianity and Judaism.

We believe that van Buren's one covenant theory will not be accepted by the Jewish community. Van Buren views the relationship between Judaism and Christianity symmetrically: Judaism must refer to Christianity in order to (fully) define itself, in order to (fully) tell its story; and Christianity must refer to Judaism in order to define itself, in order to tell its story. The more traditional understanding of the relationship between Judaism and Christianity is that it is asymmetrical: Judaism can define itself without ever referring to Christianity (this is the gist of the Rosenzweig quotation with which we started this section). But the reverse is not true; rather, Christianity must refer to Judaism in defining itself. We would like to suggest an alternative to van Buren's one covenant theory that maintains the asymmetrical relationship. We would like to suggest viewing the Jewish and Christian communities as telling overlapping stories, with the Jewish story being the basis on which the Christian story gets told.

3. An Alternative to van Buren's One Covenant Theory.

In *Christ in Context* van Buren suggests that the story of Jesus, which both presents Christians with the immediacy of God and guides the church in the way of its behavior, was told and can only be told in the context of Israel's story. This view, along with the view that the story of Jesus itself is a story of Jesus in service to Israel, is, we feel, a significant contribution to the Jewish-Christian dialogue. If the church were to follow van Buren here, it would, we believe, on the one hand, rid itself of its anti-Judaic posture of the past, and, on the other, affirm the continuing validity of the people of Israel in its covenantal relationship with God; this latter is so because the affirmation of Israel by the church is a condition of its own identity — if Israel is not in covenant with God, then neither is the church.

But the problem is that with van Buren's one covenant theory the story of Jesus is a part of Israel's story; it is a new chapter in the story that began with Abraham. The consequence of this is that Israel in reciting its story must recite, as part of it, the story of Jesus! And, again, this just will not do. Our task then is to somehow hold on to van Buren's contextual view, while letting go of his one covenant theory.

Our suggestion is this: Van Buren's one covenant view is one covenant only from God's point of view. God is the only one who remains party to the covenant throughout the story's many chapters. Certainly Israel has a covenantal point of view, but it is Sinaitic, not Abrahamic. Likewise, the church has a covenantal point of view, but its perspective is Post-Easter, not Abrahamic. Certainly both communities have a view of Abraham, but such views are from Sinai or Easter. It is only God who could have a continuous perspective beginning with Abraham, and so it is only God who can see the covenant as one.

Nevertheless, there seems no reason why we cannot keep a version of van Buren's contextual view. It might look something like this: The church's recitation of its story will depend on it first hearing Israel recite its story. If we agree with van Buren, this is an unfinished story and so is in continual need of being revised and told again. The church must wait for Israel to recite its story. There will be no chapter in that story involving Jesus. That story the church tells. After Israel first tells its story, then the church tells its story, using Israel's story as the context in which alone it can make sense of its own story. Van Buren's view would require Israel to identify with the church. Our view would require Israel to relate to the church. Instead of the church saying to Israel that both are a part of the same story, on our view the church would have to say to Israel, "Tell us your story." Such a view seems to retain the church's need of Israel, a need expressed by van Buren's contextual view, while not requiring Israel to understand the church as a part of its own story, which is a requirement of van Buren's one covenant theory.

As a Christian, van Buren's method of formulating a theology of the Jewish-Christian reality is to listen to the Jewish witness to itself beginning with the Hebrew Bible, to affirm what he hears, and then to add to it the Christian witness. But this method falters at least at one point, and that is at the point of the Abraham story found in the Jewish text. It is here that van Buren gives an interpretation of the text that he has not heard from the Jewish witness. In other words, he gives a Christian interpretation of the text: Jesus Christ is the fulfillment of God's promise to (the Gentile) Abraham that he would be the father of many nations. Van Buren knows that the Abraham story as it relates to the church is a Christian interpretation and not a Jewish one. But his hope is that it will become also part of the Jewish witness, part of the

Jewish tradition. That it is not, or, that it has not been, van Buren believes, is because of the church's anti-Judaic tradition. If the church had not developed an anti-Judaic tradition, but rather had understood itself more as Paul understood it — as a way in which God had included Gentiles into the covenant — then the Christian interpretation of part of the Abraham story would have been a part of the witness of Israel. The anti-Judaic tradition was a mistake. The Gentile-inclusion view was the view intended by God. But van Buren also argues that if the church were now to give up its anti-Judaic tradition and were to begin to understand itself according to the Gentile-inclusion view, according to his one covenant view, then Israel might yet acknowledge the Christian interpretation of the Abraham story, might yet accept the Christian understanding of the Abraham story as part of its own witness (van Buren 1983, 144-5, and 148). This argument of van Buren is not unlike Martin Luther's argument that the Jews would convert to Christianity once the hopelessly corrupt church was reformed. Van Buren argues that the only thing keeping Israel from accepting the Christian message as part of its own witness is the church's mistaken anti-Judaic tradition. Martin Luther argued that the only thing keeping Jews from converting to Christianity was the corrupt church. But Luther was proven wrong: The Jews did not convert to Christianity with the Reformation.[5] We do not believe that Israel will accept the Christian message as part of its own witness, even if the church were to give up its anti-Judaic tradition. But we also believe that it is not necessary that it do so. Instead of a one covenant view, we suggest overlapping stories. For the overlapping stories view, the Christian interpretation of the Abraham story is an interpretation produced by and meant for the Christian community. It is a story Christians tell, not a story Israel tells, not a story Israel needs to tell.

According to Rosenzweig, as we saw, even though Judaism and Christianity labor at the same task (share the same hope), world redemption, they do so with eternal enmity existing between them; and this by the intent of God. For van Buren, the antagonism between the two faith communities was not God's intent; indeed, such antagonism was a mistake. Van Buren believes God intends that Jews and Christians be mutually supportive partners in the task and hope they share. And van Buren hopes that what God intends might some day be a reality. We suggest that it is more apt to happen if Judaism and Christianity are viewed not in terms of van Buren's one covenant theory, but in terms of two communities whose stories overlap in an asymmetrical way. We believe that our overlapping covenants model of viewing Judaism and Christianity would be more acceptable to the Jewish community than van Buren's one covenant theory.

The greatest weakness of van Buren's one covenant theory seems to be that it provides too strong a linkage between the two faith communities; the linkage is that of identity. We believe that this weakness is also found in Eckardt's one covenant theory. In terms of Eckardt's one covenant theory, as we saw, Christians are characterizes as participants in the election of Israel, and as members of the household of Israel. A Jewish response to van Buren's one covenant theory might be: "The Christian story is not a part of my story." A Jewish response to Eckardt's one covenant theory might be: "Christians might be considered guests in the household of Israel. But, if this is so, it is because Jews have invited them; and remember this, guests leave, and good guests, at any rate, don't overstay their welcome. Christians might be considered guests in a Jewish household, but they are not part of the family. They are not participants in what makes Israel Israel: its election. In other words, we do not believe that the one covenant theory of Eckardt would be any more acceptable to Jews than would van Buren's one covenant theory, and for the same reason: the linkage it requires between Judaism and Christianity is too strong.

Unlike the one covenant theory which provides too strong a linkage between Judaism and Christianity, the greatest weakness we found in the two covenant theory was that it did not provide for any significant theological linkage at all. The claim of the two covenant theorists, at least those that we have considered, is that Judaism and Christianity are two different religions, separate and independent of one another. For Ruether the Jesus story reduplicates the Exodus story, the two faith communities parallel each other, and they come together, if at all, only at the End. For Ruether, once the church was founded, once the church gained its foundational paradigm, Jesus, it appropriated the (Jewish) biblical past based on that paradigm, and went into the future on its own terms. It gave the biblical past a Christian interpretation, and viewed its present and future in Christian terms. In other words, the linkage between Judaism and Christianity is at best historical. One might put it this way: Judaism and Christianity share the same root, the same biblical heritage. But what does this linkage mean for the present or the future? The two covenant theorists might accept an asymmetrical relationship between Judaism and Christianity. But if so, in defining itself Christianity's reference to Judaism would be an historical reference: Christianity emerged from Judaism. But once Christianity emerged from Judaism, it became an autonomous religion, a religion independent of Judaism. Christianity's dependence on Judaism is an historical dependence. The question is, does the two covenant theory do justice to the relationship between Judaism and Christianity? Isn't the linkage too weak between Judaism and Christianity in the two covenant theory?

Van Buren claims that the church of today cannot make sense of itself without considering itself within the context of Israel; and, it is not ancient Israel that he means here, he means Israel of the present. Van Buren believes that if the church acknowledges the eternal covenant between God and Israel, and the church came to understand itself in the context of that covenant, then it must continue to (or, once again) understand itself in the context of Israel. For van Buren the church rests on the foundation of the Christian revelation, but that revelation has a context, namely, Israel. The church's context is the story of Jesus. But the story of Jesus has a context,too; the context of Jesus' story is Israel's story. The church exists in a context that itself has a context. What this means is that Israel remains of theological significance for the church. Israel provides the context in which the church continuously comes to an understanding of itself. The church has a theological dependence on Israel. Israel provides the context in which the church formulates its own self-understanding.

We believe that van Buren's contextual view of the relationship between Judaism and Christianity is a better view than that of the two covenant theory. For the two covenant theory the church's context is the Christian revelation, which rests on its own foundation. The dependence of the church on Israel is an historical one: The church emerged from Israel. If Israel had not existed, the church would never have come to be. For van Buren the relationship between Judaism and Christianity is theological. The church is theologically dependent on Israel.

The problem is that van Buren articulates his contextual view of the relationship between Judaism and Christianity in terms of his one covenant theory. This is a problem because we have found reason to believe that van Buren's one covenant theory would not be acceptable to the Jewish side of the dialogue. Consequently, we have attempted to replace it with what we have called an overlapping view of Judaism and Christianity; a view we believe might be more acceptable. It is a feature of van Buren's one covenant theory that Israel understands the Jesus story as part of its own story. This feature is removed in our overlapping theory: Israel tells its story, then the church tells its story using Israel's story as the context in which the church's story gets told. This means that, while the feature that makes van Buren's one covenant theory unacceptable is removed, the feature that we feel is the strength of van Buren's view is maintained. Judaism is theologically important for the church today. Judaism is the context in which the church makes sense of its own story. There is an asymmetrical relationship between Judaism and Christianity. Judaism can tell its story without mentioning the Church's story, but the reverse is not true. There is an overlapping relationship between Judaism and Christianity. Theologically, the church exists in the context of Israel.

We believe that the one covenant theory provides linkage between Judaism and Christianity that is too strong. We believe that the two covenant theory provides linkage that is too weak. Therefore, we suggest a view we believe overcomes the feature that makes the one covenant view too strong, and overcomes the feature that makes the two covenant view too weak. We have suggested what we have called an overlapping view as a way of relating Judaism and Christianity.

We believe that our overlapping view would be acceptable to the Jewish side of the dialogue. At least it overcomes the feature of the one covenant view that made it, we think, unacceptable from the Jewish side. The question is, would the overlapping view be acceptable to the Christian side of the dialogue? Would Christians accept that Christianity is not just historically dependent on Israel, but theologically dependent on Israel? We shall give an argument in favor of the church accepting a theological dependence on Israel.

Christian participants to the Jewish-Christian dialogue believe that the church owes the Jewish people in a Post-Holocaust world at least two things: (1) an acknowledgement that Judaism is valid on its own terms, i.e. the covenant between God and Israel is eternal, and (2) to rid itself of its anti-Judaic tradition. The question is, what will motivate the church to carry through on its obligation to do these two things? One wants to answer, the Holocaust. But as the Holocaust recedes more and more into the past, the question is, will it be enough to motivate the church to change vis-a-vis Judaism? For the Christian participants to the Jewish-Christian dialogue the church's anti-Judaic tradition was a mistake. The question is, what do you replace it with? For the two covenant theorists it is replaced with autonomy and equality: Christianity and Judaism are autonomous but equally valid vehicles of salvation. In other words, you replace the church's negative reference to Judaism with no reference at all. For van Buren Israel is the fundamental context in which the church makes sense of itself.[6] For van Buren the replacement of the negative reference to Judaism by the church is with a positive view of Judaism: The church needs Judaism in order to make sense of itself. Van Buren's view would do more to motivate the church to carry through on its obligation to do (1) and (2) than would a two covenant view. More than this, van Buren's view would do more to prevent the church from ever again being a party to an event like the Holocaust. Van Buren's view would do more in making the church a party to the commitment, "Never Again."

4. Torah, Jesus Christ, and Wisdom.

Van Buren often demonstrates, particularly in *Christ in Context* that he is unaware of the role that Jewish Wisdom literature and Jewish Wisdom speculation played in what the early church had to say about Jesus Christ, and what rabbinic Judaism had to say about Torah. While he views Torah and Jesus Christ as functioning in similar if not identical ways, he does not suggest a way of relating the two main symbols of Judaism and Christianity. Indeed, the relating of the two main symbols is something that is lacking not only in van Buren's work, but in the Jewish-Christian dialogue itself. It is commonly understood that it is faithfulness to Torah and faithfulness to Jesus Christ that divides the Jewish and Christian communities. It would seem helpful then to Jewish-Christian relations if one could at least on some level relate Torah and Jesus Christ. To that end, we offer the following thesis: Just as Torah is a manifestation of Wisdom for Israel, so is Jesus Christ a manifestation of Wisdom for Christians. The plausibility of such a thesis suggests itself when one traces the development of Wisdom speculation (1) in the Tanakh, (the Hebrew Bible), (2) in noncanonical material of the Second Temple period, (3) in certain material of the New Testament, and (4) in rabbinic literature.

We begin with Job 28. The date of this material is disputed. Schimanowski, for example, dates it in the Persian period, 6th Century

B.C.E. (Schimanowski 1985, 18), while Hengel dates it in the period between 330 and 250 B.C.E (Hengel 1974, 97n289). Still, these two scholars agree that it is here with Job 28 that there is to be found the oldest Wisdom text from the Tanakh which expresses the idea of Wisdom's pre-existence,[7] and its mediating role between God and creation. According to Schimanowski, Job 28 represents Wisdom as an independent entity beside God, and as such is the first example of what he calls "reflektierten Weisheit" (Schimanowski 1985, 20).

It must be admitted that it is not all that clear that the idea of Wisdom's pre-existence and cosmic function is to be gotten from the text. The verses from which Schimanowski finds such ideas expressed in particular are vv 25-27.

v 25. When he [God] gave to the wind its weight, and meted out the waters by measure,

v 26. when he made a decree for the rain, and a way for the lightning of the thunder,

v 27. then he saw it [Wisdom] and declared it; he established it, and searched it out. (RSV)

Schimanowski suggests, based on a comparison with an ancient Phoenician idea of cosmology, that the wind, water, rain, and lightning of the thunder in vv 25 and 26 are the four primordial elements (vier Urelementen) with which God creates the world (Schimanowski 1985, 19). Then Schimanowski goes on to interpret v 27 in the following way, based on the Hebrew text: (1) 'God saw Wisdom' means that God selected it. What is interesting here is that whether God also created Wisdom is not addressed. (2) 'God declared Wisdom' means that God studied and used Wisdom as a measure. (3) 'God established Wisdom' means that God established Wisdom in its cosmic function, and (4) 'God searched Wisdom out' means God is thoroughly intimate with all of Wisdom(Schimanowski 1985, 20).

Again, it appears to us unclear whether the pre-existence of Wisdom and its cosmic role of mediator between God and creation can be found in this text,[8] although Schimanowski does indeed find such ideas expressed here. One thing is clear though, which is that in Job 28 the status of Wisdom in terms of God is not stated. Did God also create Wisdom? Such a question is addressed in the material we look at next: Proverbs 8:22-31.

v 22. The Lord created me at the beginning of his work, the first of his acts of old.

v 23. Ages ago I was set up, at the first, before the beginning of the earth.

v 24. When there were no depths I was brought forth, when there were no springs abounding with water.

v 25. Before the mountains had been shaped, before the hills, I was brought forth;

v 26. before he had made the earth with its fields, or the first of the dust of the world.

v 27. When he established the heavens, I was there, when he drew a circle on the face of the deep,

v 28. when he made firm the skies above, when he established the fountains of the deep,

v 29. when he assigned to the sea its limit, so that the waters might not transgress his command, when he marked out the foundations of the earth,

v 30. then I was beside him, like a master workman; and I was daily his delight, rejoicing before him always,

v 31. rejoicing in his inhabited world and delighting in the sons of men. (RSV)

While the meaning of the main verb in v 22 is disputed, Schimanowski believes that "erschaffen" was no doubt the original meaning (Schimanowski 1985, 29). If so, then in v 22f we have a clear statement that (1) God is Creator, and (2) Wisdom was the first thing which God created. This answers a question suggested but not addressed by Job 28. Verses 24-26 describe Wisdom as a cosmic primordial event, while vv 27-31 are concerned with Wisdom, God, and creation. Schimanowski admits that with vv 27-29 the function of Wisdom beside God in reference to creation is left in the dark.

Nevertheless, using the structure of the unit as a hermeneutical tool, he argues that the text intends to represent Wisdom as the mediator between God and creation, and in particular, between God and the human race (Schimanowski 1985, 34).

Here in Proverbs 8: 22-31 as in Job 28 we do not get an explicit expression of the idea of the pre-existence of Wisdom and its mediating function between God and creation. We need to interpret the text. Nevertheless, what at least seems implicit in these ancient texts do become more explicit in texts which follow upon them. This is particularly true of the rabbinic literature, as we shall see.

We turn now to the book, The Wisdom of Jesus the Son of Sirach (or, Ecclesiasticus), which is not a part of the Jewish canon, but was written by a Jewish scribe about 180 B.C.E., probably in Jerusalem (Nickelsburg 1981, 55). In Chapter One, vv 1 and 4, the pre-existence of Wisdom is expressed:

v 1. All Wisdom comes from the Lord and is with him for ever.

v 4. Wisdom was created before all things, and prudent understanding from eternity.

While in vv 9 and 10 creation, and particularly humanity, is connected with the Creator through Wisdom:

v 9. The Lord himself created Wisdom, he saw her and apportioned her, he poured her out upon all his work.

v 10. She dwells with all flesh according to his gift, and he supplied her to those who love him.

In Chapter Twenty-four the assertion about the connection between Wisdom and the world and humanity is deepened and further developed (vv 3,9, and 19-22). Nevertheless, the importance of this chapter lies elsewhere. In v 23 pre-existent Wisdom is identified with Torah!

v 23. All this is the book of the covenant of the Most High God, the Torah which Moses commanded us.

The impact that this bold identification by Sirach will have on both New Testament christology, as well as the rabbinic material, is enormous.

> This new contrast between transcendent Existence with God and earthly existence at a determined place and time represents an advance, which had a pioneering effect for the origins of assertions of pre-existence of New Testament christology, as well as for rabbinic texts about Torah... (Schimanowski 1985, 60).[9]

According to Schimanowski, the Jewish speculation about Wisdom (some of the material of which we have but briefly touched upon here) offered a way for Rabbinic Judaism to think about Torah. Indeed, in the rabbinic literature what would well describe Wisdom in the earlier Jewish material, now is used to describe Torah.

Aboth 3,18

> Israel is loved, since to her was given the instrument by which the world was created. Still greater love belongs to her, because it has been made known to her that she received the instrument of Creation, since it reads (Proverbs 4:2): A good teacher I have given you, do not forsake my Torah. (as cited in Schimanowski 1985, 217)[10]

Genesis Rabba 1.1 (a commentary on the book of Genesis)

> The Torah says: I was the instrument of the Holy One, blessed be He, as it regularly occurs also in the world: A king of flesh and blood built a palace. But, he built not from his own knowledge, but rather with the help of a masterbuilder. Again, the masterbuilder built not from his own knowledge, but rather, he used plans and descriptions, in order to know how he should order the rooms and doors. Likewise, the Holy One, blessed be He, looked into the Torah and created the world. (as cited in Schimanowski 1985, 219 n. 16).[11]

For our purposes there are at least two things to be noticed about these passages: (1) The pre-existence of Torah is certainly presupposed, while (2) Torah's mediating role in Creation is explicitly stated; something we did not find in the other Jewish material we considered. It is certainly quite plausible to think that the Wisdom literature of the Hebrew Bible and Second Temple period, and particularly the identification of Torah and Wisdom in Chapter Twenty-four of Sirach, provided the basis on which the rabbinic literature talked about the pre-existence and mediatory role of Torah.

We now turn briefly to the New Testament material. Here our thesis is essentially the same as the one concerning the rabbinic literature. The early church adopted Wisdom speculation found in Jewish Wisdom literature in developing its own christology — with some justification, much of the early christology evident in the New Testament could be called Wisdom christology.

Kloppenborg's thesis (which we have had occasion to mention already)[12] at least suggests that the historical Jesus is to be found within the sphere of wisdom sayings. Kloppenborg believes first edition Q depicts Jesus, along with John the Baptist, as envoys of Wisdom (Lk 7:31-35). But he believes that second edition Q goes beyond simply viewing Jesus as an envoy of Wisdom, depicting Jesus as sole mediator of revelation. He does not believe that Q christology identifies Christ and Wisdom. But he does believe that the christology that Q does express — attributing a property of Wisdom to Jesus — allowed the development of an authentic Sophia christology in later Christian tradition; for example, Jn 1:1-18, and Col. 1:15 (Kloppenborg 1978, 146-7).

There are a number of places in the New Testament in which Jesus Christ is asserted to be pre-existent and the mediator between God and creation. The pre-pauline christological hymn, Phil 2:6-11, expresses the pre-existence of Christ, and while no direct linguistic dependence can be maintained, its structure parallels that of Sirach (Schimanowski 1985, 331). Christ as pre-existent and as mediator between God and creation is expressed in the christological hymns of Jn 1:1-18 and Col 1:15-18, and may be based on Wisdom hymns. It is generally recognized that Paul walked in the thoughtworld of Jewish Wisdom literature. At 1 Cor 8:6 the pre-existence and mediatorial role of Christ is expressed, which may be based on Wisdom speculation. Indeed, Paul explicitly identifies Christ and Wisdom at 1 Cor 1:24. It is also likely that the mediation of Wisdom at Creation lies behind Heb 1: 2, 10. At the level of the Gospels, M. Jack Suggs has argued that the author of the Gospel of Matthew had identified Christ with Wisdom (Suggs 1970, 63-71). One could also argue that Philo's identification of Wisdom with the Logos, and the Logos with historical figures such as Moses, paved the way for the author of the Gospel of John to identify Jesus as Wisdom with the Logos of Alexandrian Judaism (Fiorenza 1975, 34).

Our contention is this: Just as early Christianity identified Jesus Christ with Wisdom, so did Rabbinic Judaism identify Torah with Wisdom. As Jesus Christ functions for the Christian community, thus does Torah function for the Jewish community. Our thesis could be stated this way: Jesus Christ is a manifestation of Wisdom for the Christian community, just as Torah is a manifestation of Wisdom for the Jewish community.

5. Conclusion.

Van Buren's "A Theology of the Jewish-Christian reality," would be of value if for no other reason than this: so far, it has gone further than any other Christian work in meeting the requirement of the church's recent confession concerning Judaism. The church has recently confessed that the covenant between Israel and God is eternal. To take seriously this confession is to work through its implication, namely, the need of the church to reformulate its own self-understanding. The confession means that a systematic reformulation of Christianity vis-a-vis Judaism is called for. At this time van Buren's work has gone further than any other Christian work in attempting to meet this call. This fact alone reflects the conviction with which van Buren works, and the concern he has both for the church and for Israel.

Would the work he has done find acceptance with the parties to the Jewish-Christian dialogue? We have argued that it is only those Christians open to the Jewish-Christian dialogue in the first place who would even consider van Buren's Post-Holocaust view of Christianity; or, at least those Christians open to considering Christianity in other than traditional ways.

We believe that van Buren's worldview owes a great deal to James; indeed, James may be the dominant influence on van Buren in this area. Particularly, the element of risk in the covenantal enterprise that precludes a message of assurance, van Buren seems to have borrowed from James. We do not find it in worldviews similar to van Buren's, except in James. We have argued that it is essential to Christianity and Judaism that there be some confidence that God will make things turn out right in the end, i.e. world redemption will be reached. In other words, we believe that a no guarantees worldview would be unacceptable to both the Christian and the Jewish communities.

If the no guarantees feature is removed from van Buren's worldview, then it seems to us that in terms of an after-life there is not a significant difference between this-world and other-world Christianity. We have argued that van Buren's notion of this-world Christianity is compelling. It is compelling to think that Christian acts of loving kindness are the stuff (not the only stuff) by which the world is being completed, by which the world is being redeemed.

Van Buren has many positive things to say about Judaism. The very premise from which he works — the covenant between God and Israel is eternal — would be applauded by many Jews. Because van Buren stresses the divine election of Israel, and Torah observance as the means by which Jews are sustained in the covenant, his views may be more warmly received by conservative Jews than by liberal Jews. In any event, we have argued that while Jews may indeed appreciate many of the positive things van Buren has to say about Judaism, they would reject the way he envisions the relationship between Judaism and Christianity; they would reject his one covenant theory. They would do so because it entails a relationship that is too strong, requiring Israel to view Christianity as a part of its own testimony, a part of its own story with God.

We attempted an alternative to van Buren's one covenant theory, which we called an overlapping view of the two religions. It is an asymmetrical view of the relationship in which is removed the feature that made van Buren's one covenant theory unacceptable. Nevertheless, our overlapping view maintains van Buren's position that Christianity is dependent on Judaism. The question is, would Christians ever accept a view of Christianity that is forever dependent on Israel? We argued that a church that viewed itself this way would be better able to rid itself of its anti-Judaic past, and better able to be a party to the commitment, "Never Again." Finally, for van Buren the central symbols of the two faith communities represent different revelations to different faith communities. Still, he never attempts to relate them; indeed this attempt to relate Torah and Jesus Christ is lacking in the Jewish-Christian dialogue itself. We have attempted to demonstrate that the Wisdom myth was used by both communities to say something important about their central symbols respectively. Then based on this demonstration, we suggested that Wisdom was manifested to the different communities in different ways: to Israel Wisdom was manifested as Torah, to the church Wisdom was manifested as Jesus Christ.

Notes:

Introduction Notes:

1. During this twelve year period, van Buren also did some work on the thought of William James. But because the influence of James on van Buren's own thinking is carried over into his Jewish-Christian dialogue period, we shall wait to consider the Jamesian influence on van Buren until we reach the appropriate place in the material produced during the dialogue period.

Chapter One Notes:

1. That Christ's coming negates or abrogates the ancient rites of Israel is the more traditional Christian anti-Judaic interpretation. Calvin adds a twist to it.

2. The traditional Protestant view of the Fall, here represented by Calvin, is that it completely cuts us off from God. Van Buren, himself a Protestant theologian, accepts this view at this point in his career. In his Jewish-Christian dialogue period, as we shall see, his view on the fallen nature of humanity changes.

3. See, for example, John Hick, "Theology and Verification," in *Theology Today*, Vol XVII, No. 1 (1960), 12ff.

4 Van Buren is writing in the early 1960s. Then as now there was no concensus on the historical Jesus. His picture of the historical Jesus is based on his reading of Bultmannian scholars who were involved in the "new quest" of the historical Jesus; for example, E. Fuchs, "Die Frage nach dem

historischen Jesus," *Zeitschrift fuer Theologie und Kirche*, 1956; and, G. Ebeling, Die Frage nach dem historischen Jesus und das Problem der Christologie," *Zeitschrift fuer Theologie und Kirche, Beiheft I*, 1959.

5. In terms of the categories, exclusivism, inclusivism, and pluralism (see Alan Race, *Christian and Religious Pluralism: Patterns in the Christian Theology of Religions.* (Maryknoll 1983) for an explanation of these categories.) van Buren seems to be moving from a position of exclusivism in *Christ in Our Place* to in some sense a position of inclusivism in *The Secular Meaning of the Gospel.* We have argued that in terms of his own position, van Buren could have moved to the position of pluralism.

6   Van Buren claims that the theological "right" has been influenced by insights of biblical theology, and so might be satisfied with his "call" and "response" Christology, which is also based on those insights. Van Buren mentions as a monument of biblical theology, The Theologisches Worterbuch Zum Neuen Testament, and he uses G. van Rad's *Das erste Buch Mose*, and Oscar Cullmann's *The Christology of the New Testament* in formulating his christology.   What van Buren means by bibical theology perhaps is the theologies that contemporary biblical scholars were discovering in the Bible.

7. See also Paul M. van Buren, *Christ in Our Place*, p. viii.

8. Looking back at *The Secular Meaning of the Gospel* from the vantage point of his Jewish-Christian dialogue period, van Buren criticizes himself for taking as normative the secular culture of his own day. See Paul M. van Buren. *Discerning the Way.* (New York: The Seabury Press, 1980), p. 58.

9. Van Buren here is relying on Wittgenstein. See Ludwig Wittgenstein. *Philosophical Investigations.* (New York: The Macmillan Company, 1953).

Chapter Two Notes:

1. Marcel Simon. *Verus Israel.* (New York: Oxford University Press, 1986) p.385. This is the central thesis of *Verus Israel.* It is opposed to Harnack's view that Judaism during this period is withdrawn and indifferent, which Simon claims Harnack assumes without any evidence. Simon's view is closer to that of Lukyn Williams, (*Adversus Judaeos.* Cambridge: Cambridge University Press, 1935). Clark Williamson (*Has God Rejected His People?* Nashville: Abingdon, 1982), John Gager (*The Origins of Anti-Semitism.* New York: Oxford University Press, 1983), and Rosemary Ruether (*Faith and Fratricide.* New York: The Seabury Press, 1979) accept Simon's thesis.

2. See James Parkes, *The Conflict of the Church and the Synagogue, A study in the Origins of Antisemitism.* (New York: Atheneum, 1969) p.181.

3. David Novak claims that the Noachide laws were used as the criterion of Gentle righteousness during the Talmudic period, and that this was a new use for these laws. See David Novak, *Jewish-Christian Dialogue.* (New York: Oxford University Press,1989) p.32. But Novak does not cite a text in the rabbinic literature that would give direct support to this claim.

4. See, for example, Taanit 65b, Jerusalem Talmud; Pesahim 118a, Tosefta Shabbat 13:5, Babylonian Talmud.

5. See, for example, Abodah Zarah, 6a.

6. See, for example, Maimonides. *Commentary on the Misnah.* (Jerusalem, 1965) Abodah Zarah 1.3 and 4. Maimonides. *The Guide of the Perplexed.* (Chicago: University of Chicago Press, 1963) 1.5.

7. This messianic preparatory role of Christianity (and Islam) was also posited before Maimonides by Rabbi Judah Ha-Levi, an eleventh century Spanish theologian. See I. Heinemann, editor. *Kuzari.* (London: East & West Library, 1947) Chapter 4.23.

8. For Maimonides the Messianic Age was not the ultimate destiny of Humankind; that was reserved for the intellectual contemplation of the essence of God. But he did not get this notion from his Jewish tradition — he got it from Aristotle.

9. The preparatory role of Christianity for Judaism put forward by Rabbi Judah Ha-Levi and Maimonides in the 12th Century is often repeated in various forms by Jewish thinkers coming after them, particularly during the 19th century. See Walter Jacob. *Christianity Through Jewish Eyes.* (Cinncinati: The Hebrew Union College Press, 1974).

10. Katz (*Exclusiveness and Tolerance,* pp.114-128, especially p.125) and Novak *(Jewish-Christian Dialogue,* pp.53-56) differ in their assessment of R. Menahem Ha-Me'iri. For Novak R. Menahem Ha-Me'iri is concerned with evaluating Christianity in terms of the category 'the Sons of Noah' and the observance of the seven Noachide commandments, i.e. purely in terms of his own tradition. But for Katz R. Menaham Ha-Me'iri develops a theory of religious tolerance that gives positive status to other religions, going well beyond simply viewing them in terms of the Noachide laws.

11. This is a basic thesis of Katz. See *Exclusiveness and Tolerance,* especially Chapter 12.

12. See Eugen Rosenstock-Huessy. *Judaism Despite Christianity.* (Alabama: University of Alabama Press, 1969). Most of the discussion took place in a series of letters between Rosenzweig, Eugen Rosenstock-Huessy and Rudolf Ehrenberg, which are reproduced in this book. Many of the ideas formulated in Rosenzweig's letters found a place in his systematic work, *The Star of Redemption.*

13. That Jesus can be viewed as within Judaism is important to the Jewish-Christian dialogue because then the Christian anti-Judaic tradition (a tradition we will explore in the next chapter, Chapter Three) could not have begun with Jesus himself.

14. See Buber, *Two Types of Faith,* p.174, and, Martin Buber. "The two Foci of the Jewish soul," in *Disputation and Dialogue,* Frank Ephraim Talmadge (editor), (New York: KTAV Publishing House Inc., 1977) pp.282-3.

Chapter Three Notes:

1. See Helga Croner, (ed.) *Stepping Stones to Further Jewish Christian Relations:* An Unabridged Collection of Christian Documents. Stimulus Book: Studies in Judaism and Christianity, I. (New York: Paulist Press, 1977). More recently, the Presbyterian Church U.S.A. (PCUSA) adopted at General Assembly in 1987 a document called "A Theological Understanding of the Relationship Between Christians and Jews." Lambeth Conference 1988 approved and adopted a document called, "Jews, Christians, and Muslims; the Way of Dialogue," and The Episcopal Church in the United States approved and adopted at General Convention 1988 a document called, "Guidelines for Christian-Jewish Relations." These latter two documents can be found in *Christian Jewish Relations*, vol.21, no.3, 1988, pp.28-55.

2. Krister Stendahl has argued in conversation that the third "kai" in Gal. 6:16 should be translated "also".

Gal.6:16. kai osoi to kanoni touto stoichesousin, eirene ep' autous kai eleos, kai epi ton Israel tou teou.

Gal. 6:16 (RSV). Peace and mercy be upon all who walk by this rule, upon the Israel of God.

Gal.6:16 (NRSV). As for those who will follow this rule---peace be upon them and mercy, *and* upon the Israel of God.

Stendahl's translation:...*also* upon the Israel of God. The RSV leaves untranslated the third 'kai' making it appear that 'the Israel of God' refers to 'all who walk by this rule,' i.e. Christians. The NRSV is closer to Stendahl translating the third 'kai' as 'and'. Of the three translations, it is only in the *RSV* translation that one could think that Paul is referring to Christianity *as* Israel and not Christianity *and* Israel.

3. The main evidence for Jesus and Jesus traditions is the four canonical Gospels themselves. Other noncanonical evidence, e.g. the Gospel of Thomas, also has become important in recent research. The ability to get behind the text to early traditions and perhaps to Jesus himself is traditionally recognized as getting started with, (1) *Das Messiasgeheimis in den Evangelion*, by William Wrede in 1901, and (2) *Der Rahmen der Geschichte Jesus*, by Karl Ludwig Schmidt in 1919. It was this latter work that began "form criticism," the identification and study of types of material independently of the gospel as a literary unit.

4. See, for example, Marcus J. Borg. "A Renaissance in Jesus Studies." *Theology Today*, October 1988, Vol XLV, No.3, 280-92.

5. For the distinction between first edition Q and second edition Q see John S. Kloppenborg. *The Formation of Q: Trajectories in Ancient Wisdom Collections.* Studies in Antiquity and Christianity. (Philadelphia: Fortress Press, 1987).

6. It is interesting to notice the changes that Matthew and Luke make to the Markan parable of the Vineyard. For example, in Mark the sequence of the

son's death is: they took him, killed him, and cast him out of the vineyard, while in Matthew the sequence is: they took him, cast him out of the vineyard, and then killed him. Is Matthew here reflecting the fact that Jesus was killed outside the walls of Jerusalem? One further example: In Luke the son becomes the beloved son. Perhaps this is Luke's attempt to make it clearer that the son in question is Jesus, (LK 3:21-22).

7. See Ruether, *Faith and Fratricide*, pp.170-81.

8. Quoted in 'The "Adversus Judaeos" Tradition in Christian Theology,' by Clark M. Williamson. *Encounter* 39(1978), pp.280-1.

9. See Ruether, *Faith and Fratricide*, pp. 24-31.

10. See Parkes, *The Conflict of the Church and the Synagogue*, Chapters 5 and 6 for legislation concerning the Jewish people after Christianity becomes the official religion of the Roman Empire.

11. For Eckardt's view on the relationship between the Holocaust and Christian negative teaching about Judaism, see A. Roy.Eckardt, *Elder and Younger Brother*. (New York: Charles Scribner's Sons, 1967) pp.7 and 11. And *Jews and Christians*. (Bloomington, Ind.: Indiana University Press, 1986) pp.29-36. For Ruether's treatment of the subject, see *Faith and Fratricide*, pp.183-225.

12. For an assessment of Parkes' work, see the comments of Alan Davies, *Anti-Semitism and the Christian Mind.* (New York: Herder and Herder, 1969) pp.138-43.

13. Eckardt, 1967,104. While there may have been some reservations on Eckardt's part in continuing his single-covenant position (see A. Roy Eckardt, "A Response to Rabbi Olan," in *Religion in Life* 42(Fall, 1973, p.409) he continues to express the view in *Jews and Christians.* (1986), pp.73 and 85.

14. Ruether's thesis is developed in *Faith and Fratricide.* See Hare, "Rejection of Jews," for a criticism of this thesis, and "The Faith and Fratricide Discussion: Old Problems and New Dimensions," where Ruether in responding to Hare's criticism modifies her position. Both these articles are in *AntiSemitism and the Foundations of Christianity*, which is a volume edited by Alan Davies that contains a number of articles by New Testament scholars and theologians, all of them written in response to Ruether's *Faith and Fratricide.*

15. Reuther, 1979, 250. Here Ruether is claiming for Christians what Rosenzweig had reserved only for Judaism. What the two covenant theorist claims, it seems, whether such claims come from the Jewish side or the Christian side, is that a proleptic experience of the Messianic Age is an experience open to both Jews and Christians.

Chapter Four Notes:

1. It is our belief that van Buren places Christianity and, as we shall see, Judaism both in history less as a way of overcoming the weakness of Rosenzweig's view and more because of his commitment to viewing reality in

terms of history, a commitment he made before coming to the Jewish-Christian dialogue, but one that continues into this period

2. This is a part of van Buren's worldview, one of his metaphysical commitments, which will be dealt with more fully when we turn to his theology of the Jewish-Christian reality.

3. For van Buren the closed canon means that an important chapter in the story of God and God's people is closed. But the story the Bible tells continues; and van Buren maintains that the Bible itself is a witness to this. It is not the closing of the canon per se, but rather not viewing the Bible as telling a story that goes beyond it that has caused what van Buren calls a distortion in the conversation---a distortion in the theological activity of the church. For van Buren, viewing the Bible as norm for theological statements, for example, rather than as beginning and the bases for getting started in the theological task, distorted the theological activity of the church. See *Discerning the Way*, pp. 160-1, 164, and, *A Christian Theology of the People Israel*, pp. 2-9, where van Buren argues against Barth's use of the Bible as norm of theological statements.

4. See Chapter Three, p.54.

5. Van Buren is not the only one who has viewed the Holocaust in terms of revelation. See Michael L. Morgan (editor). *The Jewish Thought of Emil Fackenheim: A Reader.* (Detroit: Wayne State University Press, 1987), pp. 157-60. And, Irving Greenberg. "Cloud of Smoke, Pillar of Fire: Judaism, Christianity, and Modernity after the Holocaust," in *Auschwitz: Beginning of a New Era? Reflections on the Holocaust.* Eva Fleischner (editor). (New York: KTAV Publishing House, Inc., The Cathedral Church of ST. John the Divine, Anti-Defamation League of B'nai B'rith, 1977), pp. 22-26.

Chapter Five Notes:

1. For van Buren, knowledge of God is a confession of faith. One would make this confession based on the faith perspective gained from the Easter-Pentecost event (the Christian perspective) or from the Exodus-Sinai event (the Jewish perspective). In either case, the knowledge of God that is claimed is not first God the Creator, but rather God the redeemer. It is confessing God as our redeemer that we then go on to confess God also as our Creator. In terms of actual sequence God is our Creator before God is our redeemer. But in terms of our knowledge of God, we first come to know God as our redeemer. See *A Christian Theology of the People Israel*, pp. 52-3, 57, 61-2, 69, and 78.

2. The need for this qualification will be understood later, when we explain what determines the path that history takes.

3. One could argue that it is Rosenzweig that is influencing van Buren here. But we shall argue that van Buren's worldview, including the place of God in that worldview, is as much influenced by William James as it is by Franz Rosenzweig. Indeed, as we shall see, there is one element in van Buren's

worldview, that of risk, that is only found in James. It is not found in Rosenzweig or other Jewish thinkers with worldviews similar to van Buren's.

4. See also P.F. Strawson. *Individuals.* (Garden City, New York: Anchor Book, Doubleday & Company, Inc. 1963) pp. 100ff. Strawson is a 20th century English philosopher in the Analytic Philosophy tradition, a tradition mainly practicied in the United States and England.

5. We believe that the worldview of van Buren is more influenced by William James than by that of Franz Rosenzweig, for example, or that of Irving Greenberg. The worldview of James, Rosenzweig, and Greenberg are similar, but it is only in James' view that there is no guarantee that the goal of world redemption will be reached. See Paul M. van Buren, "William James and Metaphysical Risk," in *Theological Explorations.* (New York: The Macmillan Company, 1968), pp. 144-147. For Rosenzweig world redemption is inevitable. See Chapter Two, page 71, and *The Star of Redemption*, pp. 224 and 226. For Greenberg, the path towards world redemption is similar to an evolutionary view in which progress is assured and the promised perfection will be reached. See Irving Greenberg, "The Relationship of Judaism and Christianity: Toward a New Organic Model," in *Perspectives, Quarterly Review*, Vol.4 No.4, Winter, 1984, p. 2. And, Irving Greenberg. *Voluntary Covenant: The Third Great Cycle of Jewish History. The Third Era of Jewish History: Power and Poltics.* (New York: The National Jewish Center for Learning and Leadership, 1982), pp. 1 and 27.

6. If death is sleep, did Jesus awaken from sleep, the first fruits of those who have fallen asleep? It will be interesting to see how van Buren interprets the resurrection of Jesus.

7. It will be part of our task to consider what room if any van Buren's theology allows for other religions, that is, religions other than those of the Jewish-Christian reality. Obviously, van Buren's worldview will hinder his ability to recognize the validity of other religions that have worldviews that are in conflict with his own.

Chapter Six Notes:

1. See Chapter Two p. 37.

2. Rosemary Radford Ruether & Herman J. Ruether. *The Wrath of Jonah.* (San Francisco: Harper & Row, Publishers, 1989), p. 230. For a critical review of *The Wrath of Jonah* see John K. Roth, "The Ruethers' *Wrath of Jonah:* An Essay-Review." *Continuum*, Volume One, Number One (Autumn 1990), pp. 105-115. For van Buren's response to Rosemary Ruether's criticism of his views in *The Wrath of Jonah,* see Symposium/Why Do The Ruethers Imagine A Vain Thing? Personal Rejoinders by Alice Eckardt & A. Roy Eckardt, Emil L. Fackenheim, Franklin Littell, Paul van Buren. *Continuum*, Volume One, Number One (Autumn 1990), pp. 134-36.

3. Ruether, *The Wrath of Jonah*, pp. 61-2, 135, and 228. See also

Rosemary Radford Ruether, "Western Christianity and Zionism," in *Faith and the Intifada*. Naim S. Ateek, Marc Ellis, and Rosemary Radford Ruether, editors. (Maryknoll, New York: Orbis Books, 1992), p. 155. It is not a part of Ruether's argument, but we would like to mention here the United Nations shifting position on this issue, without going into the political reasons for the shifting. In 1975 the U.N. approved a statement equating Zionism with racism. In 1991 the U.N. voted to repeal that statement. See The New York Times, September 24, 1991, A23; and December 17, 1991, A1.

4. See *The Wrath of Jonah*, p. xiv.

5. See Conor Cruise O'Brien, *The Siege: The Saga of Israel and Zionism*. (New York: Simon & Schuster, Inc., 1986), pp. 290-4.

6. See *The Wrath of Jonah* pp. 109-112 for Ruether's view on the 1948 conflict.

7. On this point, see *A Christian Theology of the People Israel*,   p. 336

Chapter Seven Notes:

1. See Chapter One, pp.17-18, and *The Secular Meaning of the Gospel*, p. 123.

2. See Chapter One, p. 18, and *The Secular Meaning of the Gospel*, pp. 121-4.

3. See Chapter Three, pp. 54-57.

4. Van Buren's image of Jesus as an eschatological prophet stands within the tradition that goes back to Albert Schweitzer (*The Quest of the Historical Jesus*. New York: Macmillan Publishing Co., Inc., 1961.) and is represented today, for example, by E.P. Sanders. See his *Jesus and Judaism*. (Philadelphia: Fortress Press, 1985). But this view of Jesus that has been the dominant view, is eroding, and is being replaced by sapiential models. See Marcus J. Borg, "A Renaissance in Jesus Studies," *Theology Today*, Vol. XLV, No. 3, October 1988, pp. 280-92.   See also Marcus J. Borg, "Portraits of Jesus in Contemporary North American Scholarship," *Harvard Theological Review*, 84:1 (1991),pp. 1-22. Some of the sapiential models, the ones that view Jesus as having a concern with a this-worldly transformation of Jewish life, would fit better van Buren's purposes than the eschatological prophet model that he does choose.

5. Van Buren's worldview does not view God as acting unilaterally to end history; but rather, views God as acting covenantally with God's partners to bring creation to its completion. God enters into God's creation to move it along towards its goal of redemption. God does not intervene to make an end to things.

6. Even though Bultmann places Jesus completely within the context of Judaism, Jesus, nevertheless, comes across in Bultmann's treatment of him, as being anti-Judaic; see especially pp. 13 and 17.

7. See Chapter One, pp. 17-18, and *The Secular Meaning of the Gospel*, pp. 126-34.

8. See Willi Marxsen, *The Beginning of Christology*. (Philadelphia: Fortress Press, 1979).

9. For van Buren's understanding of Paul, he is particularly indebted to Lloyd Gaston. See Lloyd Gaston, "Israel's Enemies in Pauline Theology." *New Testament Studies* 28 (1982), pp. 400-423; "Abraham and the Righteousness of God." *Horizons in Biblical Theology*, Volume 2 (1980), pp. 39-68; and especially, "Paul and the Torah." in *Antisemitism and the Foundations of Christianity*, edited by Alan T. Davies. (New York: Paulist Press, 1979), pp. 48-71. Important also in the new interpretation of Paul is, Krister Stendahl, *Paul Among Jews and Gentiles*. (Philadelphia: Fortress Press, 1976); and John G. Gager, *The Origins of Anti-Semitism*. (New York: Oxford University Press, 1983). See also Calvin L. Porter, " A New Paradigm for Reading Romans: Dialogue Between Christians and Jews," *Encounter* 39-40 (1978-79), pp. 257-272.

10. For van Buren, Paul's audience is broad, the nations, i.e. all Gentiles. For Gaston, Paul's audience is narrower than that: it was made up of God-fearers, Gentiles who attempted to win salvation (enter the covenant) by observing some of the Torah. Gaston views the God-fearers as legalistic gentile Judaizers. See "Paul and the Torah," pp. 56-62

11. See "Paul and the Torah," p. 65. See also Stendahl, *Paul Among the Jews and Gentiles*, pp. 26-27.

12. The notion that Christians are adopted Jews is similar to a suggestion made by Stendahl; see "Judaism and Christianity 1," *Harvard Divinity Bulletin* 28:1 (1963), pp. 1-9.

13. Here van Buren is formulating the significance of Easter — as beginning and hope---along lines suggested by Emil L. Fackenheim; see *To Mend the World*. (New York: Schocken Books, 1982), p. 285.

Chapter Eight Notes:

1. See John K. Roth's criticism of van Buren's response to the Holocaust in *Approaches to Auschwitz, The Holocaust and Its Legacy* by Richard L. Rubenstein and John K. Roth. (Atlanta: John Knox Press, 1987), pp. 296-99.

2. See Chapter One, pp .6-8.

3. Van Buren nowhere says this, but surely God has some responsibility for the Holocaust and the Cross. After all, God created human beings capable of such things.

4. That Israel is the fundamental context of the church's christology rest mainly on van Buren's one covenant theory. See Chapter Four, pp. 82-85. Van Buren in *A Christian Theology of the People Israel* presented Jesus-as-Israel-for-the-Gentiles; see pp. 248-9, 253, and 260. But then he must have realized that if Jesus is Israel for the Gentile church, then the church has no

need of Israel itself; indeed, Jesus-as-Israel-for-the-Gentiles is a displacement theory. Therefore, in *Christ in Context* Israel as the context for Jesus replaces Jesus-as-Israel-for-Gentiles; see pp. 61-5, particularly page 65.

    5. See also *Christ in Context*, pp. 188 and 220.

Chapter Nine Notes:

    1. We recognize that our defense of van Buren against the charge that his view of Christianity is simply Judaism for Gentiles, would not satisfy Pawlikowski. For Pawlikowski, van Buren's one covenant theory is static, and what he means by this is that there is no development from the Sinai revelation to the Easter revelation. For van Buren, Torah and Jesus Christ function in similar ways but in two different communities. For Pawlikowski, the Sinai revelation was a revelation to a people, while the Easter revelation was a revelation to the individual; the two revelations compliment each other. See Pawlikowski, pp. 113-15, and 121. In other words, Pawlikowski's position is similar to that of Parkes, and therefore also open to a similar criticism. If there is a tension between the individual and the community, it exists in both communities, the Jewish community and the Christian community. The Easter revelation produced community, just as did the Sinai revelation. The difference is that the Sinai revelation produced community for a people, the Jewish people, while the Easter revelation produced community for people out of many nations.

    2. See Chapter Five Notes, p.175n5.

    3. See Chapter Two, p. 43.

    4. For a positive response to van Buren's work by an orthodox Jew, see David Novak, "A Jewish response to a new Christian Theology," *Judaism,* no.31 winter 1982, pp. 112-20.

    5. When the Jews failed to respond to the Reformation in the way Luther had thought they would, his attitude changed toward them dramatically; indeed some of the worst forms of antisemitic remarks can be attributed to him after the Jews failed to convert to Christianity with the Reformation. See Martin Luther, "Writings on the Jews," in *Disputation and Dialogue,* edited by Frank Ephraim Talmage. (New York: KTAV Publishing House inc., 1975), pp. 33-6. We are not in any way suggesting that if the Jewish community were to reject van Buren's one covenant theory, that he would respond in a way similar to Luther's. Indeed, we are confident that he would not.

    6. It is also the case that for van Buren Israel is dependent on the church. It is dependent on the church in order to completely tell its own story — the

church's story is part of Israel's story. For van Buren Israel and the church are mutually dependent. Our overlapping view changes van Buren's symmetrical view to an asymmetrical view. The church is dependent on Israel for supplying the context (Israel itself) in which alone the church can make sense of itself. There is no similar dependence of Israel on the church.

7. For a discussion of the meaning of pre-existence see Schimanowski, pp. 1-12, and, R.G. Hamerton-Kelly. *Pre-Existence, Wisdom, and The Son of Man.* (Cambridge: Cambridge University Press, 1973), pp. 1-13.

8. For an alternative interpretation to that of Schimanowski, see Gerhard von Rad, *Wisdom in Israel.* (Nashville: Abingdon Press, 1972), pp. 146-8.

9. Our own translation.

10. Our own translation.

11. Our own translation.

12. See Chapter Three, p. 57 and Chapter Three Notes p. 172 n5.

Bibliography

Alon, Gedaliah. *The Jews in their Land in the Talmudic Age.*
Cambridge, Massachusetts: Harvard University Press, 1989.

Augustine. "Reply to Faustus, the Manichean," in *Disputation and Dialogue*. Edited by Frank Ephraim Talmage. New York: KTAV Publishing House Inc., (1975).

Borg, Marcus J. "Portraits of Jesus in Contemporary North American Scholarship." *Harvard Theological Review* 84, no 1 (1991).

———— "A Renaissance in Jesus Studies." *Theology Today*, October 1988.

Buber, Martin. "The Two Foci of the Jewish Soul," In *Disputation and Dialogue*, edited by Frank Ephraim Talmadge. New York: KTAV Publishing House Inc., 1977.

———— *Two Types of Faith.* New York: Harper & Row, Publishers, 1961.

Bultmann, Rudolf. "The Primitive Christian Kerygma and the Historical Jesus." in *The Historical Jesus and the Kerygmatic Christ, Essays on the New Quest of the Historical Jesus*, translated and edited by Carl E. Braaten and Roy A. Harrisville. Nashville: Abingdon Press, 1964.

———— *Theology of the New Testament.* Vol. 1. New York: Charles Scribner's Sons, 1951.

———— *Theology of the New Testament.* Vol. 2. New York: Charles Scribner's Sons, 1955.

Calvin, John. *Institutes of the Christian Religion*, edited by John T. McNeill. Philadelphia: The Westminster Press, 1960.

Cohen, Abraham. *Everyman's Talmud.* New York: Schocken Books, 1978.

Croner, Helga, editor. *Stepping Stones to Further Jewish Christian Relations: An Unabridged Collection of Christian Documents.*

Stimulus Book: Studies in Judaism and Christianity, I. New York: Paulist Press, 1977.

Davies, Alan. *Anti-Semitism and the Christian Mind.* New York: Herder and Herder, 1969.

Eckardt, A. Roy. *Elder and Younger Brother.* New York: Charles Scribner's Sons, 1967.

———— *Jews and Christians.* (Bloomington, Ind.: Indiana University Press, 1986.

———— "A Response to Rabbi Olan." *Religion in Life* 42 (Fall 1973).

The Episcopal Church in the United States. "Guidelines for Christian-Jewish Relations," in *Christian Jewish Relations*, 21, no. 3: (1988).

Fackenheim, Emil L. *The Jewish Return into History.* New York: Schocken Books, 1978).

———— *To Mend the World.* New York: Schocken Books, 1982.

Fiorenza, Elizabeth Schussler. "Wisdom Mythology and the Christological Hymns of the New Testament," in *Aspects of Wisdom in Judaism and Early Christianity*, edited by R. Wilken. (Notre Dame: Notre Dame University Press, 1975).

Flew, Anthony. "Theology and Falsification." In *New Essays in Philosophical Theology*, edited by Anthony Flew and Alasdair MacIntyre. London: SCM Press Ltd., 1955.

Gager, John. *The Origins of Anti-Semitism.* New York: Oxford University Press, 1983.

Gaston, Lloyd. "Abraham and the Righteousness of God." *Horizons in Biblical Theology.* Vol. 2. 1980.

———— "Israel's Enemies in Pauline Theology." *New Testament Studies* 28 (1982).

———— "Paul and the Torah." In *Antisemitism and the Foundations of Christianity*, edited by Alan T. Davies. New York: Paulist Press, 1979.

Greenberg, Irving. "Cloud of Smoke, Pillar of Fire: Judaism, Christianity, and Modernity after the Holocaust." In *Auschwitz: Beginning of a New Era?* edited by Eva Fleischner. New York: KTAV Publishing House Inc., The Cathedral Church of St. John the Divine, Anti-Defamation League of B'nai B'rith, 1977.

———— "The Relationship of Judaism and Christianity: Toward a New Organic Model." *Perspectives Quarterly* 4, no. 4 (1984).

———— *Voluntary Covenant: The Third Great Cycle of Jewish History. The Third Era of Jewish History: Power and Politics.* New York: The National Jewish Center for Learning and Leadership, 1982.

Hamerton-Kelly, R.G. *Pre-Existence, Wisdom, and The Son of Man.* Cambridge: Cambridge University Press, 1973.

Hare, Douglas, A.R. "The Rejection of the Jews in the Synoptic Gospels and Acts." In *AntiSemitism and the Foundations of Christianity,* edited by Alan T. Davis. New York: Paulist Press, 1979.

Heinemann, I., editor *Kuzari.* London: East & West Library, 1947.

Hengel, Martin. *Judaism and Hellenism.* London: SCM Press, Ltd, 1974.

Hick, John. "Theology and Verification." *Theology Today* XVII, no. 1 (1960).

Jacob, Walter. *Christianity Through Jewish Eyes.* Cinncinati: The Hebrew Union College Press, 1974.

Katz, Jacob. *Exclusiveness and Tolerance.* (New York: Schocken Books, 1961.

Kloppenborg, John S. "Wisdom Christology in Q." *Laval*

   Theologique et Philosophique 34 (1978).

———— "The Formation of Q: Trajectories in Ancient Wisdom

   Collections." *Studies in Antiquity and Christianity*. Philadelphia:

   Fortress Press, 1987.

Lambeth Conference. "Jews, Christians, and Muslims; the Way of

   Dialogue," *Christian Jewish Relations* 21, no. 3 (1988).

Luther, Martin. "Writings on the Jews," in *Disputation and Dialogue,*

   edited by Frank Ephraim Talmage. New York: KTAV Publishing

   House Inc., 1975.

Mack, Burton L. *A Myth of Innocence*. Philadelphia: Fortress Press,

   1988.

Maimonides. *Commentary on the Misnah*. Jerusalem, 1965.

———— *The Guide of the Perplexed*. Chicago: University of

   Chicago Press, 1963.

Marxsen, Willi. *The Beginning of Christology*. Philadelphia:

   Fortress Press, 1979.

Montefiore, C.G. & Loewe, H. *A Rabbinic Anthology*. New York:

   Schocken Books Inc., 1974.

Morgan, Michael L. *The Jewish Thought of Emil Fackenheim: A Reader.* Detroit: Wayne State University Press, 1987.

Nickelsburg, George W.E. *Jewish Literature Between the Bible and The Mishnah.* Philadelphia: Fortress Press, 1981.

Novak, David. "A Jewish response to a new Christian theology." *Judaism*, no. 31 (winter 1982).

———— *Jewish-Christian Dialogue.* New York: Oxford University Press, 1989.

O'Brien, Conor Cruise. *The Seige: The Saga of Israel and Zionism.* New York: Simon & Schuster, Inc., 1986.

Parkes, James. *The Conflict of the Church and the Synagogue.* New York: Atheneum, 1969.

———— *The Foundations of Judaism and Christianity.* Chicago: Quadrangle Books, Inc., 1960.

———— *Prelude to Dialogue.* New York: Schocken Books, Inc., 1969.

Pawlikowski, John. *Christ in the Light of the Christian-Jewish Dialogue.* Ramsey, NJ: A Stimulus Book, Paulist Press, 1982.

Porter, Calvin L. "A New Paradigm for Reading Romans: Dialogue Between Christians and Jews." *Encounter,* 1978-79, 39-40.

Race, Alan. *Christian and Religious Pluralism: Patterns in the*
    Christian Theology of Religions. Maryknoll, New York: Orbis,
    1983.

Richardson, Peter. *Israel in the Apostolic Church.* Cambridge:
    Cambridge University Press, 1969.

Rosenstock-Huessy, Eugen. *Judaism Despite Christianity.* Alabama:
    University of Alabama Press,1969.

Rosenzweig, Franz. *The Star of Redemption.* Notre Dame, IN: Notre
    Dame Press, 1985.

Roth, John K. "The Ruethers' *Wrath of Jonah:* An Essay-Reveiw."
    Continuum 1, no. 1 (1990).

Rubenstein, Richard L. and Roth, John K. *Approaches to*
    Auschwitz: The Holocaust and its Legacy. Atlanta: John Knox
    Press, 1987.

Ruether, Rosemary Radford. *Faith and Fratricide.* New York: The
    Seabury Press, 1979.

——— "The Faith and Fratricide Discussion: Old Problems and New
    Dimensions." In *AntiSemitism and the Foundations of Christianity*,
    edited by Alan Davies. New York: Paulist Press, 1979.

————— "Western Christianity and Zionism." In *Faith and the Intifada,* edited by S. Ateek, Marc Ellis, and Rosemary Radford Ruether. Maryknoll, New York: Orbis Books, 1992.

Ruether, Rosemary Radford, and Ruether, Herman. *The Wrath of Jonah.* San Francisco: Harper & Row, Publishers, 1989.

Sanders, E.P. *Jesus and Judaism.* Philadelphia: Fortress Press, 1985.

Sanders, Jack T. *The Jews in Luke-Acts.* Philadelphia: Fortress Press, 1987.

Schimanowski, Gottfried. *Weisheit und Messias.* Tuebingen: J.C.B. Mohr (Paul Siebeck), 1985.

Schoeps, Hans Joachim. *The Jewish-Christian Argument.* New York: Holt, Rinehart and Winston, 1963.

Schweitzer, Albert. *The Quest of the Historical Jesus.* (New York: Macmillan Publishing Co., Inc., 1961.

Simon, Marcel. *Verus Israel* New York: Oxford University Press, 1986.

Stendahl, Krister. "Judaism and Christianity I.*" Harvard Divinity Bulletin* 28, no. 1 (1963).

————— *Paul Among Jews and Gentiles.* New York: Philadelphia: Fortress Press, 1976.

Strawson, P.F. *Individuals.* Garden City, New York: Anchor Book, Doubleday & Company, Inc., 1963.

Suggs, M.Jack. *Wisdom, Christology and Law in Matthew's Gospel.* Cambridge, MA: Harvard University Press, 1970.

Tannehill, Robert C. "Rejection by Jews and Turning to Gentiles: The Pattern of Paul's Mission in Acts." In *Luke-Acts and the Jewish People*, edited by Joseph B. Tyson. Minneapolis: Augsburg Publishing House, 1988.

van Buren, Paul M. *The Burden of Freedom.* New York: The Seabury Press, 1976.

———— *Christ in Our Place.* London: Oliver and Boyd Ltd., 1957.

———— *A Christian Theology of the People Israel.* New York: The Seabury Press, 1983.

———— *Discerning the Way.* New York: The Seabury Press, 1980.

———— *The Edges of Language.* New York: The Macmillan Company, 1972.

———— "Probing the Jewish-Christian Reality." In *Theologians in Transition,* edited by James M. Wall. New York: The Crossroad Publishing Company, 1981.

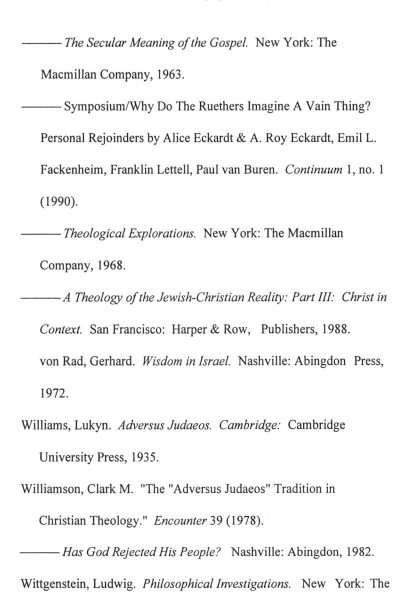

———— *The Secular Meaning of the Gospel.* New York: The
Macmillan Company, 1963.

———— Symposium/Why Do The Ruethers Imagine A Vain Thing?
Personal Rejoinders by Alice Eckardt & A. Roy Eckardt, Emil L.
Fackenheim, Franklin Lettell, Paul van Buren. *Continuum* 1, no. 1
(1990).

———— *Theological Explorations.* New York: The Macmillan
Company, 1968.

———— *A Theology of the Jewish-Christian Reality: Part III: Christ in
Context.* San Francisco: Harper & Row, Publishers, 1988.

von Rad, Gerhard. *Wisdom in Israel.* Nashville: Abingdon Press,
1972.

Williams, Lukyn. *Adversus Judaeos. Cambridge:* Cambridge
University Press, 1935.

Williamson, Clark M. "The "Adversus Judaeos" Tradition in
Christian Theology." *Encounter* 39 (1978).

———— *Has God Rejected His People?* Nashville: Abingdon, 1982.

Wittgenstein, Ludwig. *Philosophical Investigations.* New York: The
Macmillan Company, 1953.

Index